SIR GODFREY KNELLER

1. THE CHINESE CONVERT ('PÈRE COUPLET') (1687)

H.M. The King, Kensington Palace

SIR GODFREY
KNELLER
AND HIS TIMES, 1646-1723

*Being a Review of English Portraiture
of the Period*

By

LORD KILLANIN

B. T. BATSFORD LTD.
LONDON   NEW YORK   TORONTO   SYDNEY

To

D. M. T.

First Published, 1948

MADE AND PRINTED IN GREAT BRITAIN
BY T. AND A. CONSTABLE LTD., AT
HOPETOUN STREET, EDINBURGH, FOR THE
PUBLISHERS, B. T. BATSFORD LTD.,
LONDON: 15 NORTH AUDLEY STREET, W.1,
AND MALVERN WELLS, WORCESTERSHIRE.
NEW YORK: 122 EAST 55TH STREET.
TORONTO: 480-6 UNIVERSITY AVENUE.
SYDNEY: 156 CASTLEREAGH STREET.

INTRODUCTION

THIS book does not contain any startling new theories on either Sir Godfrey Kneller or his contemporaries in either late Stuart or early Hanoverian times, though it does contain a certain amount of information and some facts which have not been collected and collated previously under one cover.

My object has been to produce a brief sketch of Godfrey Kneller and his times, giving details of his career against the background of contemporary social and artistic life and showing him in relief against his competitors. I have tried to produce a book which may be of use to those who own family portraits of this period as well as to the student.

This volume begins in the reign of Charles II and ends in that of George I, when Kneller painted George II as Prince of Wales. It will be seen that quite a long and important period is covered by the active life of Godfrey Kneller.

My original research for this work began some years ago in my spare time, but in 1939, when the war started, I had to stop. As soon as possible after the end of the war I took up my researches again, but then it was not so easy. In my quest for pictures I found that some had been the victims of bombing (e.g. the portraits of Sir William Prichard and Sir William Turner in the Merchant Taylors' Hall), and that private and public collections of pictures and muniments were still not yet available owing to their having been stored during the war for safety from enemy damage or when houses were requisitioned. Also I have not been able to trace the early Lubeck pictures' fate after the war after the severe destruction, including that of the Maria Church, in that city. Further, owing to travel difficulties, I have not been able to visit all the large private collections which I had wished to see, and have had frequently to content myself with either engravings or photographs for my information.

However, I have been able to complete the book, thanks to the assistance and encouragement I have had from various sources. The advice and guidance of Sir Henry M. Hake, the Director, and Mr. C. K. Adams, the Assistant Director, of the National Portrait Gallery, has been invaluable, especially in regard to the Kit Kat pictures, although they are, of course, not responsible for any views or facts. Before their purchase for the nation by the National Art Collection fund, Lady Clinton-Baker, in whose husband's possession the Kit Kat pictures were, gave me useful help. As regards the actual research into books and manuscripts I am very grateful to the staff of the Department of Manuscripts and Prints and the Librarians and staff of the British Museum, of the Victoria and Albert Museum and the Public Record Office. Mr. Anthony Blunt, C.V.O., Keeper of the King's Pictures, and Mr. Benedict Nicolson assisted me and advised me on the pictures in the Royal Collections.

The list of all who have sent me information or assisted me would be too long to enumerate, but I would just like especially to thank the following for their help and assistance: The Marchioness of Cholmondeley, C.B.E.; The Earl of Derby, K.G.; The Earl of Mar and Kellie, K.T.; Lord Sackville, K.B.E.; Lord Fairhaven; Lady Apsley, and Sir Godfrey Thomas, Bt. Also Mr. Frank Lambert, Director of the Walker Art Gallery, Liverpool; Mr. Charles Pitman, Director of the Nottingham Art Gallery; Dr. George Furlong, Director, and Mr. Brinsley MacNamara, Secretary, the National Gallery of Ireland; Mr. James Laver of the Victoria and Albert Museum; The Secretary of the Royal Society; The Librarian of the Borough of Twickenham; The Librarians of the Bodleian and Christ Church, Oxford; Mr. A. J. Leventhall of Trinity College, Dublin; The Rev. W. P. Cole-Sheane of Twickenham; The Rev. A. T. Coldman of Henley-on-Thames; Capt. H. C. R. Brocklebank, R.N.; and The Rev. H. Dymond Peel of Donhead St. Mary.

Mr. Oliver Godfrey Kneller kindly sent me the information on the later Kneller family which is included in Appendix A.

Mrs. Katherine A. Esdaile gave invaluable advice in checking my original manuscript and making certain corrections and alterations. Mr. Robert Tredinnick has made numerous enquiries for me when I have not been able to cross to England myself.

A bibliography is contained at the end, but I would like to make special reference to *Lely and Kneller* and *Lely and the Stuart Portrait Painters*, by Mr. C. H. Collins Baker, C.V.O., of the Huntington Library, California, and formerly of the National Gallery, and later Keeper of the King's Pictures. These two works, published in 1922 and 1912, gave me my first introduction to portraiture of the period.

KILLANIN.

SPIDDAL HOUSE,
   CO. GALWAY,
      IRELAND.

CONTENTS

LIST OF ILLUSTRATIONS

ACKNOWLEDGMENT

PLATES 1, 14-22, 25 and 75 are reproduced by gracious permission of His Majesty the King. The author is indebted to the following for permission to reproduce the plates as shown:—

The Trustees of the British Museum: 4, 6, 7, 8, 12, 13, 26, 28, 34, 37, 38, 40, 41, 42, 45, 48, 59, 60, 61, 62, 63, 64, 65, 66, 67, 68, 69, 71, 72, 79, 80 and 81.

The Trustees of the National Portrait Gallery: 9, 24, 31, 32, 47, 49, 52, 54, 58, 73, 74, 77, 78, 85 and 86.

The Trustees of the Victoria and Albert Museum: 27, 29, 35, 36 and 39.

The Board of Governors and Guardians of the National Gallery of Ireland: 23.

The Board of the Nottingham Art Gallery: 56.

The President and Council of the Royal Society: 10, 11, 53, 57 and 70.

The Master and Fellows of Trinity College, Cambridge: 3 and 51.

The Librarian, the Bodleian, Oxford: 33.

The Librarian, Borough of Twickenham: 82.

The Dean and Chapter of Westminster Abbey: 76 and 84.

The Earl of Derby, K.G.: 30.

The Earl of Mar and Kellie, K.T.: 2 and 83.

The Lord Sackville, K.B.E.: 5 and 46.

The Lord Fairhaven: 43.

The Trustees of Henry, 8th Earl of Bathurst: 44.

Sir Godfrey Thomas, Bart.: 50.

The Trustees and Committee of the Garrick Club: 55.

2. FRANCES, COUNTESS OF MAR (1715)

The Earl of Mar and Kellie, K.T., Alloa

CHAPTER I

LIFE ON THE CONTINENT BEFORE 1676

THROUGHOUT the opening chapter I have spelt the name of the subject of this book KNILLER, by which name he was known until he came to England. Godfrey Kniller was born in the Hanseatic town of Lübeck on 8th August 1646.

Lübeck lies near the Baltic coast in North Germany. Until 1630, when the last meeting of the Hanseatic League was held there, this great Gothic town had flourished from the Middle Ages, since it had led the League. After the last session, sixteen years before Godfrey Kniller's birth, a definite decline had already set in and the prosperity of the citizens was decreasing.

To-day, Lübeck is full of relics of its affluent past; in 1939 it still contained five churches which were among the finest examples of Gothic Architecture with their glazed brick walls, lofty spires and tall traceried windows. The more important of them suffered severely in the bombing. These churches had been reformed since 1530 and it was in their shadow that Kniller was to pass his early years.

Godfrey was the third son born to Lucia Beuten, who had married Zacharias Kniller in the great Marienkirche on 31st October 1639. Godfrey's two elder brothers were Johan, born 15th December 1642, and John Zachary, born 6th October 1644. We know nothing of Johan and it may well be that he died as a child; of Zachary, who became a painter and accompanied Godfrey to England, we shall hear more. Three years after Godfrey's birth a fourth and youngest son Andrew was born to the Knillers. He is mentioned in Godfrey's will as being of 'Hambrough, Gent,' and we know that he was a musician and organist at St. Peter's Church, Hamburg, and also for a time organist at St. Catherine's, Lübeck.

Zacharias Kniller had led a varied life. His father, who had married into the family of Crowsen, was a large landowner near Halle in Saxony, where he was held in great esteem, and took an active part in the reformation of the church which served him in good stead. Through his friendship with the Lutheran Administrator, Zacharias was introduced to the House of Mansfeldt. The Mansfeldt family took their names from the place and flourished from the eleventh to the eighteenth century, when that branch became extinct and their lands were divided between the principalities of Saxony and Prussia. Albert, Count Mansfeldt, had been an intimate friend and collaborator with Martin Luther, who was born and died on his estate, with the result that this line of the family embraced the reformed faith whole-heartedly, though, as is well known, a cadet branch supported Charles V. One of the Mansfeldts had been furnished with an army

I

by James I of England to regain the Palatinate during the Thirty Years War, but this expedition had failed. As the result of his Lutheran contacts, old Kniller had been appointed Surveyor-General of the Mines and Collector of Revenues to the Mansfeldts, in the former capacity looking after the surface salt-mines and deeper coal-mines which produced a soft brownish fuel; the combination of the two produced the Mansfeldt wealth and revenue. Godfrey Kniller's grandfather was therefore a man of position. He owned estates and earned wealth by filling two salaried posts for which he must have been well remunerated.

Zacharias Kniller was born in 1611 on his father's estate at Eisleben, some twenty-four miles north-west of Halle. It appears that the family left here when he was a boy, probably on account of the wars, but Zachary went to Leipsic University and on leaving there proceeded to Sweden, where he was employed for a number of years, probably as an engineer or estate manager, by the old Queen Eleanor, widow of Gustavus Adolphus of Sweden. He remained with the Queen until her death, when once again he returned to Germany and married, settling at Lübeck.

Although he had been brought up on his father's estate and trained as an engineer, Zacharias had a strong penchant towards music and arts. He found himself in Lübeck leading the life of a dilettante. As his son Godfrey was to discover later, the study of mathematics and engineering, on the technical side, is very closely connected with the study of the arts. In 1657, Zacharias was appointed surveyor to the great St. Catherine Church, an architectural curiosity owing to its raised choir caused by the high vaulted crypt. At the same time he was employed as the organist—probably, as so often happens nowadays, an unremunerated and part-time hobby. He also played on the famous early sixteenth-century organ with its fine casing and its thirty-two stops, which was destroyed by bombing during the 1939-45 war. This latter was properly his parish church, as is proved by the baptismal entries of his children.

Zachary Kniller, besides having a small income from his father's estate, also had a pension from Queen Eleanor of Sweden; in between his official duties he devoted his time to painting, as is also recorded in the Church registers. Works of his were still to be seen in Lübeck before 1939; they included a well-executed portrait of Canon Caspar von Kobring in the dome of the Church of St. Catherine, Pastor Senator Helms in St. Peter's Church, and the Superintendent Hunnius in the Maria Church, besides two full-length portraits of the Rector and Chief Librarian of the town, Johan Kirchman, who died in 1643, and Town Councillor von Weisnau, who died in 1645; these hung in the Schaunhausen Library in the town.

It was in these surroundings that young Godfrey Kniller was brought up as a child. Conscious all the while, no doubt, of the continual wars that were raging throughout Europe, and perhaps inspired by stories of Gustavus Adolphus told by the old Queen, Zacharias decided that his third son, upon whom he lavished the most interest, should be trained as a soldier. Young Godfrey had already proved himself in the schoolroom as a very confident and pushing, if not unpleasantly precocious, boy; he had been taught the classics by a tutor in Lübeck who considered him above the average as a scholar; all this went to confirm Zacharias in his views of his third son's future. Frau Kniller, as was, and is, the custom in Germany, seems to have had little say in the matter.

In wandering around the magnificent and majestic old town with its fine architecture, Godfrey must have spent much time in the churches with his father when he visited them to ensure that they were being properly kept up. Lübeck at this time had no picture gallery, though most of the churches had interesting mural paintings, including the *Dance of Death* in the Maria Church, which depicted twenty-four dancing couples linked together by death. Young Godfrey also studied painting and he could watch his father at work on the portraits of the town and church dignitaries who then led the social and intellectual life of the city after the great merchants had begun to move elsewhere.

In about the year 1660, when Charles II was returning to the throne of England, bringing with him all the pomp, vanity and licentiousness of the French Court of Louis XIV, young Godfrey Kniller packed his belongings in a chest and crossed the Elbe and the Weser to make his way to the great University of Leyden, where he was to study 'Mathematics particular to fortification.' Leyden was the leading University of North-West Europe. It had been founded just under 100 years previously and its teaching was devoted to liberal thought; it was the University on which had been based the foundations of Utrecht, Gröningen and Harderwick at the beginning of the seventeenth century. When young Kniller went there, the influence of Janus Douza, who had set the very high standard of both professor and of student, was still strong. Here at Leyden, Godfrey met students from all over the world and was able to exchange views. He met a few liberal Italians who told him of the beauties and wonders of Rome and Florence; and only a few miles away, at Amsterdam, old Frans Hals and Rembrandt, surrounded by their pupils, were painting their last masterpieces.

During the time he was at Leyden, Kniller felt an overwhelming desire to study painting. His study, like that of his father in engineering, gave him helpful instruction and he learned a great deal about construction, measurements and design which was to be of use later; but as his mind developed he soon decided that his student's satchel should carry the brush of a master and not the baton of a marshal. During the vacations he would return to Lübeck, sometimes sailing round from the Dutch coast through the Baltic, but more often than not making the long journey by coach. At home he would discuss painting with his father, who was by now quite a considerable expert, and eventually persuaded him that next time he returned to the Low Countries it should not be as a military student but as a painter. Kniller never regretted the change. Later, when he was to paint famous generals such as Marlborough or De Ginkel, he would often say very pompously that he himself would have made a great marshal; be that as it may, he remained a painter.

In the year 1668 or thereabouts, for we have only the word of his journeyman and assistant Edward Byng, some fifty years later, the young Godfrey went off to Amsterdam to study under Ferdinand Bols, the pupil of Rembrandt. It has been stated that he worked under Frans Hals, but this master died in 1666 and it would appear that Hals, who was recognized as a great master in Godfrey's lifetime, would have been constantly hailed by Kniller as his master had he worked under him, whereas he only claimed the advice of the then lesser known Rembrandt when discussing his early training with Byng.

Ferdinand Bols (who must not be confused with Hans Bol the Flemish painter, 1534-1593) was born at Dordrecht in 1611. He went to Amsterdam as a student and studied under Rembrandt, with whom he remained as copyist and imitator until 1660, when he began work on his own. He had married one Elizabeth Dell in 1653 and died and was buried in Amsterdam in 1680. His pictures are represented in the great galleries of Europe. His major works are historical, biblical or straightforward portraiture; he has the firm line and design of Rembrandt, and many of his works might easily be mistaken for those of the master. In England he is represented in the National Gallery by the *Portrait of an Astronomer* signed and dated 1652; in Liverpool by *An Angel Appearing to Hagar*; in the Fitzwilliam by a portrait. In Ireland the Dublin National Gallery has his *David's Charge to Solomon*. There is a self-portrait in the Rijks Museum in Amsterdam.

Rembrandt, or Rembrandt Harmensz van Rijn to give him his full name, died in October 1669, which meant that Godfrey overlapped some two or three years with him in Amsterdam. It is true that after 1660 Rembrandt's output dropped considerably, but there are pictures painted by him which can be traced to this last period. They include *The Prodigal Son*, now in Russia, painted about 1668, the *Portrait of a Family* at Brunswick, and others in private collections. The date of his birth is uncertain, but at the earliest it was 1603, which meant that when Godfrey arrived, though he may have been ailing in health, Rembrandt was no more than sixty-three at the most. Of his influence I shall have more to say later, but after studying the drawings of Rembrandt and Godfrey I find a school likeness, and I would quote the genre and pose, such as Rembrandt's *Portrait of the Artist* in the National Gallery, as forerunner of the Kit Kat pose, although I do not know whether our artist saw this work.

Though Godfrey was working in Bols's studio, the latter must have taken his young pupil from Lübeck to visit the master at his house in Breestraat. Rembrandt too had studied in Leyden and they may have exchanged anecdotes of their University days.

Godfrey returned to Lübeck from studying painting in Amsterdam and brought with him many good canvases. It is not quite clear whether his brother Zachary accompanied him to Amsterdam, but they appeared inseparable. John Zachary shows signs of having had a classical education as a painter; it may well be that he continually followed in his younger brother's wake. Father Zacharias was well pleased by his son's progress, and, unlike many fathers of art-loving sons, was firmly convinced that Godfrey was a great genius. An army career was now quite forgotten.

Till this time all North-West Europe had been influenced by the Dutch and Flemish school of painting, but the works of the great Italian masters were now finding their way across Europe as communications improved. Zacharias was well versed in the works of Raphael and the great Italian masters, and thought his son should go south for further experience. It has been stated that Godfrey was seventeen when he went to Rome, but I think he was nearer twenty-four or even older, for he had already a full academic education and had spent some years in Amsterdam. He therefore went off to Rome with his brother Zachary in about 1670—or perhaps even in 1672, as Vertue and Horace Walpole state.

In the Imperial and Papal City he made his way first of all to the studio of Bernini. Giovanni Lorenzo Bernini was a sculptor and architect who sometimes painted portraits as his father did before him; his self-portrait is in the Uffizi Gallery in Florence. When Godfrey arrived at his studio Bernini—or Chevalier Bernini as he was known in France—was already an old man, for he had been born in Naples in 1598. Under Bernini the young Godfrey studied architecture for some little time, which further assisted him in his training in design and proportion. During this time he would wander around the city sketching the great classical buildings, ruins and statues.

From Bernini's studio he moved to that of Carlo Maratti (or Maratta), the Roman portrait painter. Maratti had been born in Ancona in 1625, but at the age of eleven arrived in Rome to be trained as a painter; and except for a short visit to Ancona between 1640 and 1650 all his work was done in that city. He had studied under Andrea Sacchi, who had trained him in the school and tradition of Raphael, Guido Reni and the Caracci. During his early years Maratti had found himself painting many pictures of the Holy Family, which had earned him the name of 'Carluccio delle Madonne,' but a few years before Kniller's arrival in Rome, Sacchi had obtained him a commission to paint a picture for the Baptistery of the Lateran, where he is represented by *Constantine Destroying the Idols*. After this he was recognized as a great master, and when Kniller entered his studio he was one of the leading and most sought-after painters in Rome. He was patronized by Pope Alexander VII and later by Pope Clement XI and King Louis XIV, who made him a Court painter. Maratti died in 1713; his *Portrait of a Cardinal* may be seen at the London National Gallery; at Hampton Court his *Virgin and St. Francis* hangs, and his *Europa* is in the National Gallery of Ireland.

After a year or more in Rome, Godfrey, who was self-confident, vain and very conceited, considered that he was now a fully trained painter, but he had not yet studied in the Venetian school, so he decided to go north to Venice where he could set up a studio of his own, planning to accept commissions and at the same time to continue a little study of that school.

In Venice he had an almost immediate success, and rapidly earned a name as a painter of historical pictures and portraits. He was first of all patronized by the Garstoni family, most of whom he portrayed; he was then introduced to Cardinal Bassadona, whose portrait he painted. This was such a success that a copy was immediately commissioned, and as soon as it was finished it was dispatched to the Vatican, where it still hangs. Venetian society of the early 1670's was parochial in that once accepted as a good painter, success was ensured. The Garstoni family recommended him to other well-known Venetian families such as the Donatos and Musingos, who employed the young portrait painter.

In Venice he heard that his father was ailing and so decided to voyage towards home, where he thought he might be able to ply his art. On the way back he stopped to paint in Nuremberg and in due course settled in Hamburg, only forty miles from Lübeck. In Hamburg his painting had a great vogue. He was taken up by one Jacob de Boe, a keen amateur of art, who owned a valuable collection of paintings which he had inherited from his brother at Leyden. This collection was made available to Godfrey, who was thus enabled to study the works of Gerard Dou and Frans van Mietis, at the same time carrying on his practice as a portrait painter.

Godfrey Kniller might well have remained in Hamburg, but on 4th April 1675 he heard news that his father had died. He hurried back to Lübeck for the funeral, and there the brothers all met. After Zacharias Kniller's estate had been settled up, Godfrey and Zachary Kniller talked of their future plans. Godfrey had already established himself as a local painter, but Zachary had not been so successful, although he had obtained a few commissions of a hack nature, such as completing the sixth picture of a set of grisaille which one Deleval had started on the pillars of St. Catherine's Church.

Godfrey had liked Italy, the climate and the country suited him, and he decided he would return to Venice, or perhaps to Rome, where the opulent merchants and prelates were always ready to commission works with which to adorn their palaces and refectories. The two brothers embarked on their trip, but as they had planned to remain permanently in Italy, they thought it a good idea to complete their European travels beforehand by visiting England. De Boe, who had patronized Godfrey in Hamburg, was a merchant having considerable trade with England, so Godfrey told him of their plans and they were immediately offered introductions. At the end of 1675 the two brothers embarked on their voyage back to Italy via France and England, Godfrey bearing in his pocket a letter from De Boe to one Jonathan Banks, a wealthy Hamburg merchant in London.

Although many pictures were painted and many must still exist, works by Kniller during the period before his visit to England are not numerous. Of the technical and artistic development I shall have more to say later; let it suffice to note that he had been trained in Amsterdam in the tradition of the school of

Hals and Rembrandt, in Italy in that of Raphael and the Caracci, as good a background, surely, as any artist could wish.

The earliest picture that can be traced hangs in the Lübeck Town Library. It is a portrait of an Aged Student and was painted in 1668, perhaps when he was studying in Amsterdam, or perhaps during one of his visits home; it has been called *Copernicus*. There is an interesting counterpart to it called the *Youthful Scholar* which is signed J. Z. K. and must have been painted by Zachary at much the same time. There are other reports and attributions of work by Godfrey during this early period, and these include large scriptural and historical subjects, but nothing is very definite. A picture called *Cornelius Bruyn* hangs in Amsterdam which some believe to be earlier, it certainly appears to date from this period.

The next traceable work is that of *Cardinal Bassadona*, painted in Venice in 1672/73 and now in Rome. It must have been about this time that he did the self-portrait which now hangs with the Dyce Collection in the Victoria and Albert Museum in London.

There were, before the war of 1939-45, though it is impossible to trace their position at the time of writing, several pictures of the post-Venice and pre-England period in Lübeck. In Maria Church there were two full-lengths—one of which is definitely by Godfrey, called Mayor *Heinrich*, in half-Spanish dress, and another, an oval, more doubtful, of Senator Frederick B. Rodder. In the same church there was also a picture which was put there as a memorial to his father after his death. It shows Zacharias Kniller when still quite a young man wearing clipped goatee beard and whiskers; the brow and chin have been damaged (this was recorded as long ago as 1845), and it is signed and ascribed as follows:

ARTIFICI ZACHARIAE KNILLER PER ANN 16 TEMPLI HUJUS STRUCTORI INDUSTRIO INVIDIAE DOMINO NON SERVATO, HATO ISLEBIL THURING a 1611 d 16 Nov donato d 4 April a 1675 vidua et filii morientes possuerunt, Johan Zacharias and Godofridos Kniller f anno 1676.

Below is the coat of arms with helmet and hawk.

The family of Heintze auf Niendorf owned certain pictures that were most certainly by Kniller; this collection included two oval portraits of *Senator Th. Fredenhagen* and his wife, both dressed in black, she wearing a dress with blue-and-white trimmings and pearls, whilst he is in wig and ruffles.

There is no doubt his family name was Kniller. This is confirmed by the registers at the Maria and St. Catherine Churches, on the inscription of the picture of Zacharias Kniller and all records prior to 1676. However, he is known to the world to-day as Godfrey Kneller, although what may have been the cause of the change of this one letter I do not know. To be consistent with contemporary records we shall refer to the family as Kneller from the time of his arrival in England, for as such he became universally known.

CHAPTER II

ENGLAND IN 1676

WHEN Godfrey Kneller and his brother John Zachary set foot in the house of Jonathan Banks in London some time early in the year 1676, they must have been struck by the caricature in England of the life of the French Court which they had seen on their way through France.

Sixteen years previously, Parliament had summoned Charles back from fifteen years' exile. This exile had been largely spent in the Court of Louis XIV. It was therefore natural that any boy who had lived his formative years in such surroundings should bring with him to England many of the customs and frills of France. Charles II was at heart a typical Englishman who loved his sport. He was a good tennis-player, fond of hunting, and thought nothing of walking from his Palace of Whitehall to that of Hampton Court. He was, however, very lazy except where sport was concerned; in 1667, when the Dutch Fleet sailed up the Medway to burn his Royal ships which had been laid up owing to Court extravagance, he was chasing butterflies. The news did not disturb him, for he merely continued his butterfly hunt, remarking: 'Naturally I am more lazy than I ought to be.' He was very indolent in all matters of state business, but had a tremendous interest in the arts and learning; we have the works of Wren and the Royal Society as testimonies of the fact. At heart he was a Roman Catholic, for that had been the religion of his mother, a French princess, and the Court of France, but he was too lazy to trouble much about this when his real religious views involved him in difficulties, and he always preferred appeasement to anything else. His brother James, Duke of York, who was to succeed him, had made a good name for himself as a general and sailor, and when Kneller arrived he had recently retired from the Admiralty. James was an abler man than Charles, but he had not his wit and gaiety, he was a fervent Roman Catholic, and his private life was much more creditable. It was said by a contemporary that 'The King could see things if he would, the Duke would see things if he could.' The result was that Charles II retained his throne for twenty-five years, reigning during the last four as absolute monarch. James too tried this, but only reigned for four years in all. Whatever one's personal political and religious convictions may be to-day, the England of the years of Kneller's arrival was not above reproach.

A short résumé of the historical events at home during this period is necessary, so that the political rivalry and intrigues which Kneller was to witness during his life in England under five monarchs may be fully appreciated.

After the Restoration, England had a Cavalier Government which at the beginning was pre-eminently Royalist and Anglican. It was led at first by Clarendon, whose daughter Anne Hyde married James II as his first wife, then by the 'Cabal' of five Ministers, and at the time of the arrival of the Kneller brothers by Danby. During the early period prior to 1668, what has become known as Clarendon's Code became effective. This began with the Act of Uniformity under which all clergy and schoolmasters had to take an oath accepting the new Prayer Book; those who refused to do so were deprived of their livings, into which they had, after all, been inducted by Cromwell and by the Five Mile Act, and they were forbidden to preach within that distance of their former parishes. This resulted in secret meetings which brought about the end of the Code, and the passing of the Conventicle Act, forbidding all dissenting religious meetings. Clarendon was dismissed. His unpopularity was increased by his intrigues as father-in-law to the heir apparent, whilst England was swept by the Plague, London by the Fire, and the Medway by the Dutch Fleet. Charles had considerable influence over the 'Cabal,' and in 1672 he announced a Declaration of Indulgence which removed all penal laws against Roman Catholics and Dissenters. This was not approved by Parliament, and immediately countered by the Test Act calling upon all who held office under the Crown to take the Sacrament according to the rites of the Anglican Church. The Duke of York retired from the Admiralty, and Clifford and Allington from the Cabal ministry, in consequence. Charles then dismissed Shaftesbury, the Ashley of the Cabal, and the Cabal came to an end.

Danby, who succeeded, was an Anglican, and Charles did not again attempt to restore or favour Catholicism during this period. It was, however, a time of intrigue during which Louis XIV was at one time subsidizing the opposition against the King, and at another bribing the King to prorogue Parliament. Charles's French mistress, Louise, Duchess of Portsmouth, was at the height of her power. This intrigue was due to the Government being more devoted to the House of Orange, whilst the opposition did not wish to force war on France. Then in 1678, just two years after the Kneller brothers had arrived, Titus Oates started a rumour of a Catholic plot to murder the King, who had not the strength of his religious convictions, and to place James on the throne. Informers— malicious and lying—sprang up everywhere; Roman Catholics at every turn were convicted; a counterplot arose by which Shaftesbury planned to divert the succession from James, Duke of York, to the Duke of Monmouth (who, as we shall see in the next chapter, was responsible for Kneller's first successes in England). The Duke of Monmouth was an illegitimate son of Charles II, but Shaftesbury's party produced alleged proofs of the Duke being legitimate.

Between 1679 and 1680 three short Parliaments were held at Oxford. These were the last occasions on which members had to attend fully armed, for feeling was running very high. An Exclusion Bill was introduced by these Parliaments to place Monmouth on the throne on Charles's death instead of the Duke of York. Charles said he would prefer his son to be hanged rather than legitimized; he had his way, and the Bill was still unpassed in 1681. From then until his death, Charles was supreme and the Duke of Monmouth was banished.

Politically, the interesting feature of this period is, that in it lies the beginning of the party system in politics. Party members were at first known as Petitioners and Abhorrers—the former wishing to petition Parliament and the Abhorrers not wishing to interfere with the King's prerogative. They very shortly afterwards became known as the Whigs and Tories. The origin of the word Whig has been in dispute, but it may well be from the Scottish Covenanters' motto 'We hope in God,' whilst Tory is derived from 'Tar a Ri' ('Come, O King') associated with the creed of the Irish native levies enlisted in the civil war on behalf of the Royalist cause; the parties later became the Liberals and the Conservatives, the one being progressive and the other fostering stability. In 1681 both parties were strongly opposed to anything pertaining to Roman Catholicism, but the Whigs were in agreement with freedom at least for the dissenters, whilst the Tories considered that the Anglican Church was the only legitimate Church. When James II came to the throne, he was opposed by both parties alike. No sooner was he King than the Duke of Monmouth attempted to seize power. He landed in Dorset but was defeated at the Battle of Sedgemoor and taken prisoner, tried and beheaded. Following the rising, all his followers were arrested and tried by Judge Jeffreys, who rid the King of these rebels at the Bloody Assizes, but by doing so infuriated the country as the news, grossly exaggerated, travelled through the land. The final blow to James's future as monarch came in 1688. His wife, Mary of Modena, gave birth to a son, which ensured a Catholic line, for he had only two daughters by his first wife Anne Hyde—Mary, who was to become Mary II, and Anne, who was to succeed Mary in 1702. This son James was to reappear as the Old Pretender, and in 1688 came the Revolution.

It was against this historical background that Kneller found himself called on to paint in his early years, though he was to live not only to see the complete development of the party system but also that of the office of Prime Minister, when in due course the House of Hanover came to the throne in 1714 with a king who knew little and cared less about England.

As all historians have found, it is very difficult to describe any scene other than a none too flattering one of the rule of the later Stuarts. It was an age of scepticism and intolerance, but has also been called by writers of history the Age of Dryden, and that name is an apt one. During it flourished John Dryden, whom Kneller painted on several occasions (3 and 4); there is a three-quarter-length in the National Gallery and a recently acquired half-length in the Hall of his old College, Trinity, Cambridge. Dryden was the leading literary figure of the age and his *Absalom and Achitophel* is the best commentary on its politics, but it was also the age which produced Newton's *Principia*, Milton's *Paradise Lost*, Purcell's music, Wren's churches, and Locke's (70) philosophy.

Charles brought with him from France very Gallic customs, which appeared all the more conspicuous after years of Puritan rule under the Commonwealth.

3. JOHN DRYDEN

Trinity College, Cambridge

4. JOHN DRYDEN

Engraved by J. Faber, Senior (1708)

5. WILLIAM WYCHERLEY

Lord Sackville, Knole

During that period the theatres of England had been closed, as they were considered a bad and immoral influence. No sooner had the monarch returned than they were reopened. Here, as in painting, architecture and costume, the French influence was felt, for Charles had lived in the age of Molière, Corneille and Racine; but, like the manners of the Court, everything was exaggerated to the extent of caricature. The most successful play at the time of the Knellers' arrival was still *The Country Wife*, written by Wycherley in about 1673. Wycherley, too, became a friend of the painter and there is a good portrait of him at Knole Park, Sevenoaks (5). In *The Country Wife* the hero pretends to be a eunuch so that he may enter the chamber, which enables him to seduce a lady. If this subterfuge was to be admired, as was indeed expected, it only goes to show that the state of mind of the people was a little warped; but there were a few revivals of Ben Jonson and Shakespeare. The age of Vanbrugh (as a playwright) and Congreve was to follow some ten years later. It is interesting to note that after the Restoration women replaced boys in female parts and in consequence Kneller was one of the first artists to paint actresses—whom, like the actors, he frequently represented on his canvases, as, for example, Anne Oldfield (55) at the Garrick Club.

In 1676 the Royal Society had become an important and powerful influence. It met every Wednesday in Arundel House, lent by the Duke of Norfolk after the Society had had to leave Gresham House, which was required as a civic building following the Fire of London. Newton had been elected a Fellow in 1671, and Wren, who had previously been a lecturer, was to be chosen President ten years later. The Society, which Charles benefited and encouraged in every way, exchanged views and correspondence with all the philosophers of Europe, besides encouraging research in science, learning and the arts at home.

London in 1676 was as yet small. The fire which had swept through in 1666 still left its mark and there were many places within the City which were not rebuilt. Wren had been commissioned by Charles II shortly after his Restoration, and before the fire, to prepare plans for the reconstruction of St. Paul's. He had started work on a plan which was something akin to St. Peter's. Wren himself described it as 'after a good Roman manner, not like the Gothic rudeness of the old design'; the plans are still preserved at Oxford. To-day we should have admired the Gothic rudeness which was to be built, but we were perhaps fortunate to be spared the first Wren building with its heavy dome on heavier pillars, this dome in its turn surmounted by another smaller one and a spire. The King approved the design but the Chapter did not. It was shelved, and then the Great Fire swept through the City, leaving only part of a shell near the choir.

In 1673 Wren was approached and ordered to produce a fresh plan; this he did, and much to his disgust it was not accepted. There is a model of it at the London Museum, but Charles gave him permission to deviate from the plan at his will without reference to the authorities. The result was the present Cathedral, which is a model of magnificence and design. When the Knellers arrived the burnt remains had been pulled down to the ground, the crypt had been gutted and the new foundations were starting to bear the cathedral church, the first stone of which was laid on 21st June 1675. The wharfs, where now Billingsgate Market stands, were crowded with barges bringing stone from Portland, whilst Wren lived in the house on the South Bank on what is now known as Cardinal's Wharf, watching the new city and cathedral rise. The choir was opened in 1697 and the whole in 1710. At the same time Wren was erecting fifty-four other churches in the City, stretching from west of Leicester Fields to Bow, all with spires and towers. He had planned to rebuild all the City with wide roads ranging from St. Paul's, but, as was so often the case, until legislation in recent years, the City or public authorities had no power of compulsory land purchase. So alongside the magnificent building of Wren went the commercial building by the merchants anxious to regain their homes, offices and warehouses. In 1676 the City was a complete wreck. The Monument was erected and on top there was to be a statue of Charles II, to whom more statues were erected than to any other sovereign save Victoria; however, a flaming urn, which is still there, was substituted. Outside the City gates new groups of houses were everywhere rising, and gradually the village of Westminster was being joined by the westward growth of London; highwaymen and robbers lurked between Paddington and Covent Garden. The King and his Court lived well away from the City at Whitehall, and should anything bring them up to the Tower or City, they usually went by barge, for the road leading from Charing Cross opposite Wallingford House to Temple Bar was very bad. The Dutch-born architect, William Winde, a pupil of John Webb, was building in the area of Lincoln's Inn Fields, Dr. Barebones in Bloomsbury, otherwise Wren was supreme, for the age of Vanbrugh, architect as well as playwright, had not yet arrived. Vanbrugh was a boy of twelve in 1676, growing to adolescence to be trained as a soldier. The influence of the Court in architecture was predominantly French, for although Wren drew most of his ideas from Italy, he knew Bernini, who had been Kneller's master, and went to discuss the rebuilding of London with him when Bernini was on a visit to Paris in his official capacity as adviser to Louis XIV. Wren was very anxious to copy Bernini's colonnaded arcade of St. Peter's, thinking this would look well around the close of St. Paul's, but the Italian would not let him have the plans to copy.

The centre of fashion as far as those living in private houses, other than in large demesnes such as Clarendon's home in Hyde Park, was beginning to converge round Drury Lane and Bow Street besides stretching along the riverbank between Whitehall and Somerset House. All the area which is now known as Lambeth and Waterloo was marshland. St. Thomas's Hospital stood on the road to Rotherhithe and Woolwich; London Bridge, then and for long afterwards the only bridge across the Thames, led from Gracechurch Street to St. Saviour's, Southwark; between London Bridge and the Marsh was the Paris Garden and Bear Garden. All the traffic from the south, including that from Dover, came into London this way (6 and 7).

Of the painters at the time of Godfrey Kneller's arrival I shall write at some length. Suffice it to say that the grossness of the Court resulted in the flattering portraits of ladies at which the prim might well look askance, seeing them depicted as goddesses and shepherdesses (though certainly neither), dressed in the skimpiest of dresses with breast and back bare for all to see; the fashion gave the draughtsman who liked his line and curve and the colourist who liked his flesh pigments a great opportunity. It was perhaps a pity that Etty did not live almost two centuries earlier, for he might well have done justice to the fashionable ladies of the time. The example was set by the Royal mistresses, Portsmouth and Cleveland, the lesser nobility following suit. Like the painters, the Court poets, when they were not satirizing the religious and political feuds of the day, squandered much of their talents in imitations of the classics, as their flowery, allegorical and often too flimsy verses show.

I have tried to give some idea of the historical and contemporary cultural background which greeted the two German brothers, but I must go into a little more detail regarding costume, for like everything else it was at first influenced by France. It is also the very key to the dating of pictures, besides being responsible for the colours and pose of the works of Godfrey Kneller.

As the question of dress is complicated, I shall first go into detail of the man's attire and then that of his consort. Godfrey Kneller on arriving in England would first of all be struck by the great variety of colours that he would see at the Court and in the town; east of the Rhine men's dress was much more sombre. If he met a man about town getting out of his coach after a short journey, for he would rarely travel afoot, he would be wearing a low-crowned black hat, cocked perhaps at one side, bordered with metallic lace or silk trimming and decorated with large coloured plumes. This hat was worn on top of a formal long wig which was a mass of corkscrew curls. The face might be slightly painted, and he might have a patch or two. Unless he was elderly or old-fashioned, or perhaps a courtier, he would be clean-shaven, though some of Charles's courtiers, like some of the elder men, might have a slight moustache. He would wear a tunic and vest (just about this time they began to be called coat and waistcoat), which had replaced the doublet, now only worn by soldiers after the time of the Restoration.

The coat was cut straight to below the knee; it would be easy fitting, with sleeves turned up at the elbow into broad cuffs and slit to the hip on either side, the slits being trimmed with dummy buttons. The coat would fasten in front from neck to hem but was usually worn open; the pockets were vertical or horizontal and placed below the hips; the waistcoat was always of the same length and probably of the same material as the coat. The waistcoat was buttoned all the way down and its long sleeves tightly cut to appear below the short coat-sleeve. The shirt might show at the collar and certainly at the sleeves, its cuffs being garnished with ribbon and lace. The throat opening was often edged with a frill of ribbon or lace, whilst a cravat of lace, or a neck-cloth, had now replaced the falling bands of an earlier generation.

Breeches were full and gartered at the knee, whilst the long stirrup hose, which might be adorned with ribbon and lace gartering, went up under the breeches. The breeches were never of the same colour or material as the coat, being usually black, whilst the stockings were of any colour. On his feet a man would wear either a light jack-boot caught in by a buckle, button or lace to the small of the leg or the ankle, or shoes which were just coming into fashion. He might have a cluster of ribbons as a shoulder-knot. The sword-top would appear under his coat carried on a broad shoulder-belt, the sword being of the short type worn with Court dress to-day, and the handle would be decorated with ribbon. There might be a broad sash over the coat, or under the coat and over the waistcoat. If he was very smart, a lace pocket-handkerchief might protrude from a pocket or cuff, whilst he might carry a tall malacca cane tied with ribbon.

After Kneller's arrival, and chiefly during the period prior to 1700, this clothing adapted itself more and more to that which we are more accustomed to associate with the early eighteenth century, when the hat became cocked on all three sides, the feathers disappeared and the metallic ribbon was replaced by a lace or feather edging. The wig remained for a while much the same length, but by the beginning of the eighteenth century towered above the brow in two peaks. Shorter wigs were worn for travelling, and after 1680 soldiers and others tied their back curls, and later the whole, with a bow at the nape.

The coat and waistcoat began to be more shaped—more like a frock-coat; in fact, the waistcoats became shorter and lost their sleeves; coats became waisted and their backs fanned out; coat-sleeves gradually became longer and large cuffs came into fashion, though the turn-up vanished after 1710; only two or three waistcoat buttons were done up to allow the shirt to be seen; the cravat became longer and had either more lace or else none at all.

The breeches lost their bagginess, and before the turn of the century they were plain-cut, buckling below the knee with the hose worn over the bottom of the breeches, being kept in position by a plain garter. The ornamental buckle on the shoes had come in and grew in size during the first decade of the eighteenth century. Large leather leggings (spatter-dashes) were worn, especially when riding.

Throughout this period the 'cavalier' cloak was only worn for travelling.

Women's dress is harder to define at any period, for then as now fashions changed very rapidly. Between 1670 and 1680, for instance, at least three different popular types of hair style can be traced. The typical coiffure had side curls hanging close to the face, with a growing tendency to adopt long curls brought from the nape forward over the shoulders. Another fashion was a close crop of curls all over the head, whilst a third was known as the 'bullhead' and consisted of a mop of curls over the forehead only. The hair was usually uncovered, though a kerchief or head lace might be worn; and the hair over the ears was adorned with ribbons, which developed into loops of ribbons across the crown. This, a decade later, developed into the fontange (or tower) and eventually became the lace cap.

6. 'THE EAST PROSPECT OF LONDON, SOUTHWARK AND THE BRIDGE'

From an engraving by Sutton Nicholls (circa 1720), British Museum

7. LONDON FROM SOUTHWARK

From an engraving by F. de Wit (circa 1680), British Museum

8. A STUDY OF HORSES

British Museum

The basis of woman's dress was the bodice, a tight-laced corsage baring the shoulders but with full elbow-sleeves often gathered in tight pleats at the armhole, and fastened either in front or more often behind with large bows or jewellery. Sleeves had ceased to be puffed after about 1670, whilst the elbow might be finished with a fringe of ribbon loops.

The skirt was pleated into the waist and opened to expose the petticoat. A very fashionable lady might wear a gown—this had just come in, for previously only a loose cloak referred to as a 'sack' had been worn; the gown had a separate bodice and was worn closely shaped to the body. Little linen was shown, and the high collar had not been worn for fifteen or twenty years. The bare shoulders and neck might be veiled with a scarf, and the upper border of the chemise might protrude above the bodice.

The shoes, either of needle-point, satin, brocade or leather, were very elaborate. The heel was high and the toe pointed, though square-toed shoes appear after 1680. The arms would be covered by long elbow-gloves or mittens and a long stick or parasol might be carried.

During the last two decades of the seventeenth century the 'fontage' came in, to diminish and vanish about 1710. This was a close linen cap worn at the back of the head, ornamented in front with upright graduated tiers of wired-out lace and ribbon nodding over the face, and at the back had long lace lappets that would be pinned up; over it could be worn a hood or kerchief. This fashion reached its peak about 1700, but Kneller rarely painted women with this grotesque head-dress, preferring the earlier modes. At the time of his death, the fontange had been reduced to a cap.

About 1690 the bustle (cul-de-Paris) had come in, but by 1711 hoops had replaced the bustle. The dresses during this period were decorated with lace and ribbons and the fashionable shirt trailed on the ground.

In the 1680's the hair on top was dressed in a curly mass on either side of a centre parting. In all these coiffures it forms a small bun at the back, while long corkscrew ringlets fall down behind or are brought forward over the shoulder. During the 1690's it is built high in front, generally forming two towering peaks.

After 1690 aprons were much worn for decoration and display; and in the latter part of the century, long scarves had come in for outdoor use. Later, ladies powdered their hair and with this fashion went an increase in the use of paint, and their clothing became even more elaborate until the reign of Queen Anne, when there was a general decline in detail and ornament until the reign of George III.

CHAPTER III

HIS EARLY YEARS IN ENGLAND UP TO 1702

IT is stated by George Vertue and others, that the Kneller brothers arrived in England as early as 1674; I am doubtful about this assertion, which was based on a report by Byng at the time of Kneller's death saying how long Godfrey had been in England. We know that the picture of his father in Lübeck was not sent to the church until 1675; although it may have been painted before and sent over from England, there seems no reason to believe that the brothers arrived earlier than 1676. Godfrey had already gained for himself a small reputation in Nuremberg, and a considerable one in Hamburg and Lübeck, and this could not have been done in a few months after their return from Italy. It would therefore appear that the brothers left Lübeck to return to Italy via France and England not earlier than late in 1675. On the way they stopped in Paris, and probably arrived in London some time in 1676.

The brothers planned to make a short tour of England to study the great collections in English country houses, especially the works of Van Dyck. Godfrey had now established himself as a portrait painter, and the more he could quote of the world-famous masters of the past the more successful he was likely to be.

The brothers travelled by coach from Dover and drove into London over London Bridge to Mr. Banks's house. From the London Directory it would appear that Jonathan Banks, to whom the brothers had their letter of introduction, then lived in Fenchurch Street. The brothers on arrival here informed their host that they would only be staying a short time. No sooner had they settled in than they were asked to draw and paint his family. These portraits, his first works in England, I cannot trace. One day they may be traced, but as his style was to develop very rapidly, it may be more difficult to authenticate them.

Mr. Banks was a friend of Mr. James Vernon, who was secretary to the Duke of Monmouth, and the Duke, as mentioned, was the King's bastard son, whom certain political elements claimed legitimate. Mr. Vernon would often call at the Banks's house, and somewhere about the end of 1676 he saw Kneller's pictures of Mr. and Mrs. Banks. He was delighted, and immediately requested that Kneller should paint his portrait. This picture has now been found (9) and was recently purchased by the National Portrait Gallery, where it hangs to-day. It is very thinly painted, and shows Vernon as a bust in an oval; his head is inclined to the left and he wears the full curly corkscrew wig and long lace cravat of the time. James Vernon was later to be Secretary of State to William III from 1697 to 1700; he came from Staffordshire, and was the father of the famous Admiral Vernon.

16

9. THE HON. JAMES VERNON (1676-77)

National Portrait Gallery

D. SAMVEL PEPYS ARMIG.
REG. SOC. PRÆSES. AN°. 1684

10. SAMUEL PEPYS (1684)

JOANNES EVELYN ARMIG.
REG. SOCIETATIS SOC.

11. JOHN EVELYN (1685)

The Royal Society

12. JAMES II

Engraved by J. Beckett

Vernon was greatly pleased with this picture and returned to tell his master. At this time Monmouth was extremely busy, but intimated that he would like to be painted by the new German painter. Godfrey Kneller was delighted with his success, and although he spoke little English, though speaking German, Italian or extremely bad French, he decided that there might be better opportunities of making a living in England rather than in going on to Venice. His brother was agreeable, and with the help of Banks they found accommodation in York Buildings, but this was only to be a temporary home, for commissions started to come in, with the result that they moved to Durham Yard, where they remained until 1681. They then moved to the fashionable Piazza at Covent Garden, where they remained until the death of John Zachary in 1702 (81); he is buried in the neighbouring church of St. Paul's, Covent Garden.

It has been claimed that the brothers went to Italy again in 1677, the grounds for this claim being that George Vertue in his very full and detailed Notebook [1] says he saw a picture of a *Roman Amphitheatre* at Kneller's house which was dated 1677. This might account for a short gap in reports of the painter's progress in England, but I am very doubtful. We know that when he was working with Bernini he did many sketches and drawings of Roman architecture, and it would surely be more likely that this was a picture worked up from such sketches and painted in his studio, either to pass the time or as an idea for a background. I do not think that he visited Italy again.

During these years Monmouth was the centre of plotting, but the plans were foiled in 1679 when the Whigs were defeated at Bothwell Bridge. After this Monmouth returned for a short while to London and appears to have been on friendly terms with his father again. No sooner had he returned than it was arranged that Godfrey Kneller should paint him; this was done in the same year. There is a picture of Monmouth, one of many, in the possession of the Duke of Buccleuch, which, though some doubt has been thrown on it, is probably the first picture of Monmouth painted by the artist.

George Vertue is very critical of this picture and wrote that it was so different, or rather so much worse than those of Kneller's later productions, that a contemporary critic could not guess of whom it was done, though it was the very picture which earned him a great reputation, and was the principal cause of his continuance in England.

It is interesting in that the Duke of Monmouth was so delighted that he told his father of the work, and Charles II first sat to Kneller at the end of the year.

Peter Lely was then King's painter and had just been commissioned to paint a new state picture of Charles II for the Duke of York: Charles agreed that the young German might bring his easel to Whitehall at the same time and paint his picture too. As Kneller had already been in the country some few years, he may well have met Lely before and known his methods of work; the result was that Kneller had finished his picture before Lely had covered his canvas with

[1] B.M. Add. MSS. 23275.

the basic pigment. Lely was of course an old man, for he died a year afterwards, being buried on 7th December 1680; he was knighted after painting this royal portrait.

To give the old painter his due, he was generous with praise for his rival's picture painted in a few hours only, and the monarch was also much impressed: it is therefore not surprising that after Lely's death Kneller became the chief Court painter. As he was only thirty-four and had not been in England more than five years, this was a very remarkable appointment.

In 1684 he was again to paint the Duke of Monmouth, and Charles II as well. These pictures were sent up to Holyrood Palace to be hung with the De Witte series in the Great Gallery, and there they remained until 1708, when Queen Anne passed them by warrant to the Mar family. They are still at Alloa in Lord Mar and Kellie's possession.

The next year Kneller was dispatched to France to paint Louis XIV, then at the height of his power, and he probably took his brother with him. There is a version of this picture at Drayton, but I think the original remained in France. By the time Kneller had returned from this trip his royal patron had died in February 1685, and James II had come to the throne. Kneller had already painted James as Duke of York, but he was at once commissioned to paint the coronation state portraits which now hang in the Royal Galleries at Windsor; there are copies in my private collections. The accession of James II was immediately followed by Monmouth's rebellion and execution.

In 1687 Kneller may have gone abroad again, for there is a picture signed and dated of Louise de Kerouaille, Duchess of Portsmouth, painted this year at Sherborne. It is known that after the death of Charles the Duchess of Portsmouth immediately returned to France. Kneller, however, was so often content to paint from a sketch that I would rather think that this picture was done after that which hangs at Goodwood, which is signed and dated 1684. There is another picture of her dated 1688 at Holkham.

The year 1688 was the decisive year for the Stuart line, and Kneller was to be closely associated with it. On 10th June James Edward, the Old Pretender, was born, and on 21st June the Verney *Reminiscences* record that Godfrey Kneller painted the baby. Doubts were cast on his legitimacy by the Whigs, but Kneller had none, for he said at that time:

'Wet de devil de Prince of Wales te son of a brickbat woman, begot it is a ly. I am not of his party, nor shall not be for him, I am satisfet wit wat ye parliament has done, but I must tell you wat I am sure of, and in what I cannot be mistaken. His fader and moder have sate to me about 36 times a piece, and I know every line and bit in their faces. Begot I could paint King James just now by memory. I sayh this child is so like both, yt there is not a feature in his face, but wat belongs either to his fader or his moder; this I'm sure of, and be got, I cannot be mistaken. Nay ye nails of his fingers are his moders ye Queen yt was. Doctor you may be out in you letters but be got I cant be out in my lines.'

This was said to Dean Aldrich of Christ Church at Oxford in the presence of

13. FRONTISPIECE TO 'THE BEAUTIES'

Engraved by John Faber, Junior

15. DIANA, DUCHESS OF ST. ALBANS

H.M. The King, Hampton Court (1691-92)

14. MARY, COUNTESS OF ESSEX

17. MARGARET, COUNTESS OF RANELAGH

H.M. The King, Hampton Court (1691-92)

16. ANNE, LADY MIDDLETON .

19. ISABELLA, DUCHESS OF GRAFTON

H.M. The King, Hampton Court (1691-92)

18. CAREY, COUNTESS OF PETERBOROUGH

21. MISS PITT (later MRS. SCROOP)

H.M. The King, Hampton Court (1691-92)

20. MARY, COUNTESS OF DORSET

22. SIR ISAAC NEWTON (1689)

H.M. The King, Kensington Palace

23. EARL OF ATHLONE (1695)

National Gallery of Ireland

24. ANTHONY LEIGH IN THE PART OF DOMINIC IN THE 'SPANISH FRIAR'
BY DRYDEN (1689)

Dr. Charlett of University College; Dr. Hudson, the librarian; and Dr. Gregory, Savilian professor.

It is interesting as it shows that when he said it, probably at the beginning of the eighteenth century, his English was still very imperfect and his accent pronounced. Further, it shows that he had thrown in his hand completely with the House of Orange, but that was probably expedient for he was no politician.

Later that year, flushed with the success of a male heir to the throne and oblivious to the dangers, James II summoned his Court painter and ordered a fresh state portrait. This was started on 5th/6th November 1688, and whilst Kneller was painting the monarch news came of William's landing at Torbay. This picture was a present for Pepys, and after the news was brought him the King went on sitting because it was being done for his devoted servant.

Godfrey Kneller was unperturbed. He had owed his first success to Monmouth, who had handed him on to his father, who in turn bequeathed him to James II. Religious strife mattered little to him, for the days of painters and politics had not yet arrived.

Kneller was reaching his zenith as a popular painter and we find him painting Wren (57) who, the year before, had been elected President of the Royal Society; and also Evelyn (11), as recorded in his Diary of 6th July, these pictures being now in the Royal Society Library at Burlington House. To the same period are attributed those of Pepys at Greenwich, Newton at Kensington Palace (22) and Anthony Leigh (24), the actor, at the Garrick Club and the National Portrait Gallery.

No sooner had William settled down than Godfrey found himself in favour once more. The victors of William's war were his first subjects. He painted John Churchill after the Battle of the Boyne, and Godert de Ginkel, later Earl of Athlone, who won the Battle of Aughrim in 1691. This latter picture is in the Dublin National Portrait Gallery (23).

It was at this time that he was commissioned to paint the pictures now known as the *Hampton Court Beauties*. Horace Walpole was told by old Lady Carlisle, who remembered the event, that the idea of the Beauties was first thought of by Queen Mary during the King's absence. Lady Dorchester advised the Queen against it, saying, 'Madam, if the King was to ask for the portraits of all the wits in his Court, would not the rest think he called them fools?' However, the pictures were commissioned. Though originally twelve in number, now only eight remain. They are all full-length, as opposed to Lely's seated ladies. They represent Diana de Vere, Duchess of St. Albans; Lady Mary Bentinck, Countess of Essex; Carey Fraser, Countess of Peterborough; Lady Margaret Cecil, Countess of Ranelagh; Miss Pitt (later Mrs. Scroop); Isabella, Duchess of Grafton; Mary Compton, Countess of Dorset; and Lady Middleton (14-21). The missing Beauties are Mary II, the Duchess of Manchester, the Duchess of Marlborough and the Countess of Clarendon.

As a set they are very decorative, but as individual pictures very disappointing.

All are painted full length facing the spectator, attired in conventional drapery but without the preposterous head-dress of the period, though the hair is carefully painted not to disturb the taste. Whilst Kneller managed to depict men's characters, he often failed with his women, as shown here. The picture of the Duchess of St. Albans alone has any individuality (15).

Lord Lansdowne, who knew all the ladies, concluded his *Progress of Poetry* with the lines:

'Oh, Kneller, like thy picture were my song
Clear as thy paint, and like thy pencil strong,
The matchless beauties should recorded be,
Immortal in my verse as in thy gallery.'

As a result of his pictures of Generals and Beauties, Godfrey found himself knighted and presented by William with the chain and medal bearing the King's head which appears in all his self-portraits after this date. It may be seen in the small one with the Kit Kat series (32) and in the large last portrait at the Bodleian Library, Oxford (33), and also on his monument by Rysbrack (84). His patent is dated 3rd March 1691, when he was still only forty-five. (Lely had been knighted at the age of sixty-two, in his last year.) He is described in the patent as 'Principal Portrait Painter in Ordinary to the King.' In 1695 the King awarded him an annuity of £200 per annum, and he remained at work in England until 1697, when the King sent him to Brussels to paint the Elector of Bavaria on horseback. On this trip his brother must have been ailing, for he was accompanied only by his assistant J. J. Backer, who painted many of his draperies.

By the time of his return, William had signed the Treaty of Ryswick by which France recognized William as King of England. In honour of this occasion, Kneller painted the gigantic equestrian picture which now hangs at Hampton Court, and for which there are sketches in many collections (25).

Three years later, Count Wratistan, the Emperor Leopold's Ambassador to England, conferred on Godfrey the dignity of Nobleman and the title of Knight of the Holy Roman Empire, but it was not until 1703 that he painted the Emperor Charles VI.

In 1697 he painted Princess Anne and her husband Prince George of Denmark with their small son the Duke of Gloucester; the latter, the little heir to the throne who reached the age of eleven and died in 1701. And in consequence of his death the Act of Settlement was passed which ensured the end of the Stuart dynasty.

It will be seen that, once having entered the Royal Circle thanks to James Vernon, Kneller rapidly found himself in favour. When Queen Anne came to the throne, he had already painted Charles II (27), James II (12) and Mary of Modena, William III (66) and Mary II (67) (who would sit to no other painter), and Queen Anne (26) and her family, as well as Louis XIV and the Elector of Bavaria. These were the days when kings were supreme in the setting of fashion. Needless to say the courtiers, followed by the nobility and persons of fashion, besides the men of

25. WILLIAM III ON HORSEBACK

H.M. The King, Hampton Court

26. QUEEN ANNE

Engraved by John Simon (1702)

27. CHARLES II

Engraved by J. Smith

28. MRS. VOSS AND HER DAUGHTER

Engraved by J. Smith (1687)

art and letters, all wished to be portrayed by the 'Pictor Regis.' Godfrey Kneller's technique and development as a painter I discuss in another chapter.

During this period of early fame, Godfrey spent any spare time he had in the coffee-houses, especially those round the Covent Garden area; in these he met the leading men of the world of arts and letters. It was in the coffee-houses that the early newspapers and social commentaries such as the *Spectator* and *Tatler* were read and discussed; it was to these coffee-houses that Godfrey, accompanied by his brother, went to hear the news and views. Godfrey was something of a Vicar of Bray; as a foreigner he kept clear of all politics, but as an ambitious Court painter he was anxious to keep in with whoever might be in power. So he watched the barometer of politics, especially as they affected the monarchy.

One of the coffee-houses he visited, kept by a Mrs. Voss, was in St. James's Market. She was, like Kneller, a Hanoverian, and it is probable that when he first arrived he found the company of this compatriot pleasant, for he spoke very bad English. Mrs. Voss had been previously married to a Quaker of Austin Friars, but Kneller purchased her from her husband. Mrs. Voss became Kneller's mistress and had a child by him; she was a very beautiful woman and Kneller at this time was particularly handsome, so no wonder their daughter Agnes was a great beauty. Kneller painted her and there is a record of this painting engraved by John Smith in 1705. It shows her at half-length almost facing the spectator, and looking downwards towards an open book resting on a vase; there is a veil at the back of her head, her dress is plain, her hands are joined and her elbows rest on a table. The engraving bears the couplet

'Devotion in such looks does graceful shine
And forces us to own her power divine.'

Godfrey Kneller was to marry another woman later, but as he had no children by her he recognized this girl Agnes as his heir. She married a man called Huckle, and they had a son called Godfrey who was born in 1710.

There is another picture, also engraved by John Smith, of *Mrs. Voss with her child* (28). This is undated but would most certainly have been painted somewhere between 1685 and 1690, and shows Mrs. Voss reclining on a bank, as a shepherdess wearing a bracelet on her arm which carries a portrait of Sir Godfrey. The child stands to her right. There has been some dispute whether this child was a girl or boy, but there is little doubt that it was the daughter Agnes, for he took no pains to conceal his illegitimate child: why should he, after the examples set by successive Courts? It has been said that James Worsdale, a painter and pupil of Kneller, was a bastard son of his; this may have been the case, but it certainly was not by Mrs. Voss, and I can find no mention of the paternity of this painter. It would appear that from receipts for pictures for the years 1684-85, in the possession of Sir Gyles Isham, that Mrs. Voss was known as Mrs. Kneller and assisted in his business matters.

CHAPTER IV

KNELLER—THE MAN

THE reputation that Godfrey Kneller left behind is not very attractive, to put it mildly. Turning over a few works, I find, for instance, Edith Sitwell in her *Alexander Pope* referring to the 'fractious, vain and acquisitive Kneller.'

There is another little work called *Sir Godfrey Kneller and his Friends* which says:

'Sir Godfrey Kneller, in character and as a painter, was a complete epitome of his own days. Selfish, coarse, unimaginative and an infidel in religion, a boaster in his discourse and a wit in his conversation.'

It is the duty of a biographer to support or repudiate the theories on his subject's character, and this I will endeavour to do.

As regards his appearance, we are confined to the study of portraits and prints of the period. The first problem that arises is to identify what portraits reputed to be of Kneller do in fact represent him. It is customary to describe any picture of a painter (that is, any man holding a brush and palette or an engraving) which might possibly have been created during the years he was in England as a picture of Kneller. I have come across many such, and the majority can usually be authenticated, through comparison with contemporary engravings, as the work of other artists. They are frequently by Kneller or from his school, but more often than not represent contemporary painters such as Verrio of the famous mural painting, or Jean Baptiste Monnoyer who painted flowers, or Smith or White the contemporary mezzotinters.

There was a picture which was long identified as a self-portrait of Godfrey Kneller in the National Portrait Gallery. It was previously entitled *Isaac Newton*. Unfortunately this picture is that most often reproduced, especially in histories of painting and other works, as being of Kneller painted by himself. It is, however, no more Kneller than it is Newton. The National Portrait Gallery have sensibly not retitled it, for unless they were certain it would only be complicating the issue. If they did give it a name, they might perhaps attach the label John Zachary Kneller (31). In the original edition of Walpole's *Anecdotes* the two engravings by Chambers after the mezzotints by Beckett are reproduced—a large one of Godfrey Kneller and a smaller oval of his brother. Any attributions are usually based on this print, which, like the rest of Walpole's notes, is based on Vertue's collection of portrait drawings of artists, unhappily dispersed at the Strawberry Hill Sale (in itself rather a dangerous authority). The original painting from which Beckett made his engraving is almost certainly one of the two now in Lord Derby's possession at Knowsley, which were bought at the Strawberry Hill Sale in 1842 (30). One thing certain is that the original Walpole illustration

29. SELF-PORTRAIT (1672-73)

Victoria and Albert Museum

30. SELF-PORTRAIT (*circa* 1685)

Lord Derby

was engraved by Beckett in Kneller's lifetime from a self-portrait, for that of Godfrey was published in 1685—ten years after he came to England. Beckett's original print therefore gives us a very good clue to Godfrey Kneller's appearance when he was in his fortieth year.

There hangs with the Kit Kat collection a small three-quarter-length picture (32). It is a very small picture, perhaps copied from a larger one. This was engraved as Plate 1 in Faber's collection of the Kit Kat pictures. It represents Sir Godfrey when much older, probably painted between 1711 and 1720, and shows him in a wig wearing among other things the chain and medal presented to him by William III; in the background is his country house at Whitton, which he did not purchase until 1711. There is a large and very similar picture, possibly the original, in the Uffizi Museum at Florence; when I was last there it was not on view, but it was painted by request and sent to the Tuscan Gallery in his lifetime, where it hung in the Gallery of Painters. He is one of the few English painters, for we must call Godfrey by now an English painter, represented in the international gallery of portraits of artists. There is a similar painting—though the pose is slightly different, the colouring of the clothes not the same and the detail of the house not so definite—in the Bodleian Library at Oxford, which was given to the University by Kneller in 1721 (33). We may therefore safely assume that the Kit Kat, Uffizi and Bodleian pictures show the painter in the last two decades of his life.

We now require an early picture, and this is to be found in the Victoria and Albert Museum, where there is a picture of a youth of some twenty years of age (29). It is called *Kneller by Himself*, and after careful study of the physiognomy I am confident that this attribution is correct. The picture is of great interest as far as the development of his art is concerned, for it is one of the few examples we have, and the only one that I can trace in England, of his work before his arrival here. There is a pen drawing of a bearded man in armour in the British Museum. This may be the earliest work extant in England, dating from his student days (37).

At one time a *Crucifixion* by Kneller was sold in which he portrayed himself as Christ. This picture cannot be traced at the moment, but Lord Fairhaven at Anglesey Abbey, Cambridge, has a small *Crucifixion* measuring about 13″ by 10″ in which St. Peter is certainly Godfrey whilst I suspect the Magdalene to be Mrs. Voss; this picture is signed and dated 1686 at the foot of the Cross—at about the time, that is, of his meeting her (43). Kneller's face tallies in all respects with Beckett's engraving.

Strangely enough, or perhaps not so strange, for Godfrey may have considered that there was no one else worthy of doing the work, there appears to be no picture of him by any other contemporary artist except Verrio, who included him and Baptist May in the mural painting, since plastered over, on the staircase at St. George's Hall, Windsor; and Smibert, the portrait painter who later took the art of English portraiture to America by way of the West Indies, who included him in a *Group of Virtuosi* in 1724, but this was painted after Kneller's death.

We must judge Godfrey's appearance from his own self-portraits. It may be assumed that if anything he flattered his looks, for he was conscious of them. On one occasion he paid Sir Richard Steele the essayist the compliment of referring to him 'as nearly as good-looking a man as myself.' There is no doubt of his good looks, for they are frequently recorded.

The picture in the Dyce Collection at the Victoria and Albert is in an oval 21″ by 17¼″, with the body turned to the right, whilst the head faces half right. He wears the long full corkscrew wig lightly painted; his features are well and clearly cut, his lips a little sensuous and his eyes penetrating and intense. An interesting feature is that the angle and pose of the face is identical to the head on the three-quarter-length Kit Kat picture, and this enables the likeness to be traced and confirmed, for the ears, lip, mouth and chin are identical. In the Kit Kat picture the forehead this time appears more receding, but I think this is due to the full-dress wig, which is dressed high.

The Beckett print, which was engraved midway between the early Dyce picture and the later Kit Kat and Bodleian portraits, is a head and shoulders in an oval. Here he wears his own hair to the shoulders and faces to the left with his head half left. This is the same man as the Dyce picture and he is still good-looking, though there are signs of the face filling out, especially around the jaw-bone and chin. In the version by Chambers in Walpole's *Anecdotes*, he has a quiff of hair over his right temple.

The last pictures, with their ornate clothing, details in the dress, medal, chain and ring, show us the successful man. Here is a puffed-up peacock pouting with pride at the accomplishments which had resulted in his being honoured by royalty and accumulating a fortune from his studio.

These pictures are worth studying, for they tell their own story of progress in the subject's own lines far better than can any biographer with words. Certainly they confirm an air of vanity, but they do not give the impression of one who is unimaginative, boastful or an infidel.

George Vertue tells us a little of Godfrey's appearance and character which is borne out by anecdotes. Vertue first of all remarks on Kneller's very good looks. Then, discussing prints of him, he writes:

'This Picture has been twice done in Print so that posterity and those that do not know him personally may have some idea of this great man. Joyned to that a perfect state of health continually, a florid complexion, active, vigorous, a good memory, a pleasant conversation, finely entertaining when painting, that is always observed that his performance is with so much facility, that no seeming confinement to sitting (as is usual) that People go away with more sprightliness than they came.'

If he was boastful, vain and conceited he was at least very good company, and all the wits and nobility flocked to his studio. Unlike most painters, who hate having any other person in the studio when at work, Sir Godfrey liked as many admirers standing round as possible. In the chapter on him as a painter I write of his technique and studio methods. Here suffice it to describe a sitting at which

Alexander Pope was present and which has been handed down in Pope's own words:

'As I was sitting by Sir Godfrey Kneller one day, whilst he was drawing a picture, he stopped and said: "I cannot do so well as I should unless you flatter me a little, pray flatter me, Mr. Pope. You know I love to be flattered."

I was at once willing to try how far his vanity would carry him, and afterwards considering a picture, which he had just finished, for a good while, very attentively I said to him in French (for he had been talking some time before in that language): "On lit dans les Ecritures saintes, que le Bon Dieu faisait l'homme après son image, mais je crois que s'il voudra faire un autre à present, qu'il ferait l'image après que voilà.' (One reads in the scriptures that God made man after his own image, but I believe that if he wished to create another at the moment he would do so after the likeness of the picture that I see there.)

Sir Godfrey turned round very gravely and replied:

"Vous avez raison, Monsieur Pope, par Dieu je le crois aussi."

(You are right, Mr. Pope, by God I believe that too.)'

This little anecdote has been transposed to mean that the new image of man should be like Godfrey himself and not like this particular picture. Spence in his *Anecdotes* records it as above and I am sure this is its correct form. The story gives a very clear insight into our subject's character. The request for flattery shows that he liked it, and this is further confirmed by his serious reply; but at the same time I feel that there is a twinkle and spark of humour when, after asking Pope to flatter him, he says, 'You know how I love to be flattered.'

There is another not unamusing story which we have handed down to us in Sir Godfrey's own words. This story has also been quoted as proof of his exaggerated vanity, but to my mind it shows a man well aware of his own failings, telling a joke against himself. This incident, to have been told to Pope, must have happened, like the last one, in the last decade of his life, when Kneller had become friendly with the young poet.

I shall use Sir Godfrey's own words so that the reader may judge for himself.

'A night or two ago,' said Sir Godfrey, 'I had a very odd sort of a dream. I dreamt that I was dead and very soon afterwards found myself walking a narrow path that led up between two hills, rising pretty equally on each side of it. Before me I saw a door and a great number of people about it. I walked towards them—as I drew near I could distinguish St. Peter by his keys with some other of the Apostles; they were admitting people as they came to the door. When I had joined the company I could see several seats everyway a little distance within the door. As the first after my coming up approached for admittance St. Peter asked his name, then his religion.

"I am a Roman Catholic," replied the spirit.

"Go in then," says St. Peter, "and sit down on those seats there on the right hand."

The next was a Presbyterian; he was admitted too after the usual question, and was ordered to sit down on the seats opposite to the other.

My turn came next, and as I approached, St. Peter very civilly asked me my name. I said it was "Kneller."

I had no sooner said so than St. Luke, who was standing just by, turned towards me and said with a great deal of earnestness.

"What? The famous Sir Godfrey Kneller from England!"

25

"The very same at your service," I replied.

On this St. Luke drew near to me, embraced me and made me a great many compliments on the art we had both of us followed in this world. He entered so far into the subject that he seemed almost to have forgot the business for which I came thither.

At last, however, he recollected himself and said:

"I beg your pardon Sir Godfrey, I was so taken up with the pleasure of conversing with you, but, apropos, pray, sir, what religion may you be of?"

"Why truly, sir," says I, "I am of no religion."

"O sir," says he, "you will be so good then as to go on and take your seat where you please."'

If this may be a little profane, though not in the least for the age in which it was told, it is not unamusing. Kneller, in fact, had no religion, though he painted religious and other devotional pictures with fervour.

He could be very jealous and he did not care for competitors, except perhaps the young who had come from his studio and had been trained by him. Michael Dahl, a Swede, was painting during the same time, and though on and off Kneller was on such good terms with Dahl that he painted the latter's portrait, he could be jealous. It is, for instance, recorded that at one time he gave all possible help to Zinke, a jeweller and enameller, because he had set himself up in opposition to another enameller, Boits, who had 'spoken in favour of Dahl.'

Then at another period when he had purchased and was decorating his house at Twickenham, he had decided to employ James Thornhill to paint the staircase, but heard that Thornhill was in his spare time painting portraits. Kneller immediately withdrew the contract from Thornhill and gave it to Laguerre, saying that 'no portrait painter would decorate his house.' Further, he would occasionally boast that Peter Lely had died heart-broken at his success, but this is not borne out by the account of the two paintings of Charles II.

Godfrey Kneller also liked his food and drink, though he managed to live to a greater age than others who had the same taste. Jacob Tonson the publisher obtained pictures by a combination of flattery and bribery. Tonson flattered Kneller, telling him that he was the finest master and sending him from time to time a haunch of venison and a dozen bottles of claret.

Once Kneller remarked:

'How old Jacob loves me; he is a very good man; you see how he loves me, he sends me good things and the venison was fat.'

In point of fact it was convenient to Tonson both as secretary of the Kit Kat Club and a publisher of prints to keep in well with the master portrait painter of the day, and he had obtained many commissions for Sir Godfrey.

Jonathan Richardson in his entertaining collection *Richardsonia* adds an amusing corollary to Tonson's venison bribes. He says that one old Geekie, a surgeon, managed to obtain several pictures, including one of himself, from Sir Godfrey, but that he obtained them cheap for he only gave praises, 'but then his praises were as fat as Jacob's venison.' Richardson says no praise could be too gross for Sir Godfrey.

26

31. UNKNOWN MAN

32. SELF-PORTRAIT (*circa* 1715)

National Portrait Gallery

Geekie's son William, who had a varied career, having been an officer in the Dragoons, Fellow of Queen's College, Cambridge, and later a parson, had a little share in his father's flattery, for he wrote the following epigram:

'While meaner artists labour hard to trace
The outward lines and features of a face,
Your magic pencil Kneller takes the soul,
And when you paint the man you paint him whole.'

Some modern critics may readily agree with the last line, but not in the same sense as William Geekie, for they may deplore the many whole-length pictures as having no artistic merit. Godfrey read young Geekie's epigram and at once said: 'Send the young man to me, I'll give him his picture.'

Godfrey Kneller was a good business man and he knew well that one good deed follows another. Once he was overheard saying to Cock, the Christie of his day:

'By God, I love you Mr. Cock, and I will do you good, but you must do something for me too, Mr. Cock. One hand can wash the face, but two can wash one another.'

If Godfrey liked laughing at himself, provided that laughter was indirectly to his advantage and he originated the joke, he did not like being mocked by others. One evening at his house in Covent Garden a friend, James Craggs, brought along one Dick Escart an actor. During the evening, much to the amusement of all, Escart mimicked several eminent people, including Lords Godolphin, Somers and Halifax—all members of the Kit Kat Club. Then at the end he mimicked Sir Godfrey, who was very angry at having his leg pulled and who with his guttural accent and splutterings was doubtless an easy butt. 'Nay,' cried Sir Godfrey, 'now you are out, man, by God that is not me,' and the party came to an end.

As we know, Godfrey was trained in his youth to be a soldier. He frequently mentioned that he would have been a very good general. Certainly he liked to make himself look very martial in his later self-portraits, and Lord Cork, when seeing that in the Uffizi, had remarked that he looked 'fiercesome and by his dress and his posture seems fitter to hold a truncheon than a pencil.'

Sir Godfrey led the life of a successful man or magnate. He made much money and lived well. He was justified in his vanity. Certainly during his lifetime he had been more successful than any of his predecessors. He was the first painter to be created a baronet by George I in 1715. He lived sumptuously and according to his wealth, and had a definite position which he was determined to keep.

When, after 1711, he was living at Whitton near Twickenham he was made a Justice of the Peace for Middlesex. Most of the defendants who came before him were paupers. He was now given an opportunity to show his humanity. As so often happens with any successful or self-made man he had outwardly a streak of vanity caused by shyness, but at heart he was kind and lenient.

One of the first cases that Sir Godfrey heard was that of a man who prosecuted one of his servants for stealing some money. Kneller went into the case with great care and found that the man had taken the money which the master had purposely left lying on his table in order to test his servant's honesty. The temptation had been too much, and the servant had been easily caught by the provocative act.

Kneller immediately dismissed the case but ordered the master, who had been a witness, to be arrested and brought before him. As soon as the master was in the dock he was condemned to prison for having treated his servant thus and having deliberately put temptation in his way. This may not have been law but at least it was equity, and showed on whose side were Sir Godfrey's natural feelings.

Pope in his *Imitation of Horace*, Book II, Epistle ii, wrote as a result:

> 'Faith, in such case, if you should prosecute,
> I think Sir Godfrey should decide the suit,
> Who sent the thief who stole the cash away,
> And punished him that put it in his way.'

He sat on the local Bench for some six or eight years, and was most regular and conscientious in his attendance. It was his boast that he would never sign a warrant to distrain the goods of any person for debt; he was therefore very popular with the paupers and debtors, of whom there were many in all classes at this time.

One of the main problems that a Justice had to deal with up to the middle of the eighteenth century was created by an Act of Settlement which had been passed by Charles II's Cavalier Parliament. By this Act every parish in which a man tried to settle could send him back to the parish of which he was a native, for fear that his stay in the new abode might at a later date cause him to become chargeable on the rates. As George Trevelyan in his *Social History of England* has pointed out:

> 'Nine-tenths of the people of England were liable to be expelled from any parish save their own with every circumstance of arrest and ignominy, however good their character and even if they had secured remunerative work. The panic fear of some parish authorities lest newcomers should some day fall on the rates caused them to exercise this unjust power in quite unnecessary cases.'

This Act placed a check on the fluidity of labour, and was indeed an outrage in a free country, but it was not until the time of Adam Smith that steps were taken to remedy it. Sitting on the Bench at Twickenham in Middlesex, then the richest county in the country owing to so much of greater London being within its limit, Kneller took the law into his own hands. Cases of men were continually brought before him, usually in an effort to remove them from some parish within the petty sessional area. Godfrey never asked from which parish they came but asked which parish was the richest—that from which they came or that from which the authorities were trying to remove them. Hearing which was the richer, he would then issue an order permitting the man to be in that parish in spite of the Act of Settlement.

This shows Kneller, if not sticking to the letter of the law, at least as an early

33. SELF-PORTRAIT (1720)

Bodleian Library, Oxford

34. DUKE OF GRAFTON

Engraved by J. Faber (1731), *after Kit Kat Collection*

reformer by equity of the condition of the poorer class. As a result he was much appreciated.

But I am certain that he knew his own failings, as a story told and repeated by him shows. One day Alexander Pope and he were out together and they met a man who was a trader in New Guinea. The man was described as a nephew of Kneller's, but I think must have been some cousin by marriage.

Rather pompously Sir Godfrey said to this young man who was just back from his travels:

'You have the honour of meeting and seeing the two greatest men in the world.'

To which the trader replied:

'I don't know how great you may be but I don't like your looks: I have often bought a much better man than both of you together—all muscle and bone—for ten guineas.'

This must have been a shock to Sir Godfrey and Pope—especially the latter, who was very sensitive about his deformity. To give them each their due they both repeated the story, though I doubt if either would like to have had it repeated by others than themselves.

These self-portraits and anecdotes I think give some picture of Godfrey Kneller as a man. His looks and wit are unquestioned, his vanity and boastfulness evident, but I think they were partly justified by his success as a foreigner who had won his way from being an unknown painter, able to speak little else than German and Dutch, to a position of being sought after both for company and for commissions by all the land. At least he was conscious of his weakness. He certainly was profane and irreligious, but this did not prevent him from painting pictures of which churches are proud, or assisting them materially and financially, as for instance in the restoration of the Parish Church at Twickenham after it had fallen down. Though a little hot-blooded before his marriage, he did not disown his illegitimate child but rather claimed and honoured her and her progeny; and as far as his charity and humanity are concerned, his appearance on the Bench shows where his true feelings lay, for most Benches were filled with the rich and with landed proprietors who did not like or tolerate such overriding of the law.

Under an engraving of 1711 is written:

> 'Raphael's, like Homer's, was the nobler part
> But Titian's painting looked like Virgil's Art,
> Thy genius gives thee both, where true design,
> Postures imposed, and lively colours join.
> Likeness is ever there; but still the best,
> Like proper thoughts in lofty language drest,
> More cannot be, by mortal art exprest,
> But venerable age shall add the rest.'

This was praise indeed, and it was praise that went to Kneller's head. In the next chapter we shall discuss how far justified that praise was.

CHAPTER V

KNELLER—THE PAINTER

WHEN Godfrey Kneller died in 1723 he left behind him in his studio in Great Queen Street some eight hundred unfinished pictures which his assistant Edward Byng was to complete and sell in conjunction with Lady Kneller. That number of unfinished pictures can give some idea of the quantity which the Kneller Studio had produced between 1676 and 1723. Without visiting every house, gallery and collection in the British Isles and Ireland, besides many continental collections, it is not possible to estimate the extent of the master's work, but I think that a guess at some hundred pictures a year, making a total of some five thousand, would not be far out. It is not therefore strange to find in so great a number of pictures a very uneven standard. It is in this respect that Kneller failed as an artist. Once when he was reproached for a very bad picture he exclaimed:

'Phi; it will not be thought more, nobody will believe the same man painted these as the Chinese at Windsor.'

He was referring to a picture known as the *Chinese Convert* which was painted in 1687 and which at the moment of writing is hanging at Kensington Palace (1). It is an extremely fine piece of painting showing this young Chinaman at full-length in soutane and cap. This picture was included in the collection of Royal Pictures shown at Burlington House in the autumn of 1946.

There is a reference in Lord Clarendon's Diary for the year 1687-1688 that Père Couplet, a Jesuit Missionary, and the Chinese whom he had brought with him into England, had supped with him. Though mistaking the picture for a negro, the author of the French *Abrégé* wrote: 'On ne cesse point d'admirer le beau nègre qui est dans le château de Windsor.' Kneller knew that it was a good and well-painted portrait and as such it is recognized to-day as it was in his lifetime. This picture is often called Père Couplet, but it is, of course, of the Chinaman Père Couplet brought to England.

Critics up to the third or fourth decade of the eighteenth century are very lavish in their praise of Kneller. For instance, Buckeridge in his Life of Kneller, appended to De Pile's *Life of Painters*, says:

'His draught is most exact, no Painter ever excelled him in a sure outline and graceful disposal of figures, nor took a better resemblance of a face, which seldom failed to express in the most prevailing and to the best advantage, always adding to it a mien and grace suitable to the character and peculiar to the person he represented.'

That was contemporary criticism by one who knew the artist and the sitter. Horace Walpole, writing some fifty years after Kneller's death, thought

36. UNKNOWN YOUTH

Victoria and Albert Museum

35. UNKNOWN MAN

Victoria and Albert Museum

37. MAN IN ARMOUR (Sketch)

British Museum

38. THREE FIGURES (Sketch)

British Museum

39. DESIGN FOR A FANCY PORTRAIT (Pen and Wash)

Victoria and Albert Museum

40. THREE HEADS (Chalk)

British Museum

42. A DEER (Charcoal)

41. A GREYHOUND (Charcoal)

differently. Of course, Buckeridge could only compare Kneller with a standard set by Van Dyck and Lely for Stuart portrait painting, whilst Walpole wrote in the age of Hogarth and Reynolds; this is his verdict:

'Had he lived in a country where his merits had been rewarded accordingly to the worth of his productions instead of the number, he might have shone in the roll of the greatest masters . . . where he offered one picture to fame he sacrificed twenty to lucre.'

And a contemporary writer, Mr. R. H. Wilenski for instance, in his *English Painting* briefly dismisses Kneller with the words: 'Kneller's triumphs were undeserved.'

In recent years the most thorough research into portrait painting of the Stuart period and the eighteenth century has been undertaken by Mr. C. H. Collins Baker. The student of Technique should read his *Lely and the Stuart Portrait Painters* for a careful study of the works of Lely, Kneller and the lesser-known contemporaries.

We know that Kneller arrived in England with a classical training behind him. His masters had been found in the Dutch school of Rembrandt and Bols (or even Frans Hals some say), besides those of Naples, Rome and Venice. One would therefore look in his early work for examples of the influence of these masters. Personally I find it hard to trace. Looking through the drawings of heads in the Dyce Collection at the Victoria and Albert Museum (35, 36), or those of heads or animals in the British Museum (8, 40, 41, 42), it is quite evident that he knew how to draw well. There are signs of the firm pencil of Rembrandt combined with the study of anatomy which he followed in Italy. But looking at his early paintings, I can see no sign of the influence of Italy. His portraits up to about 1700 show the influence of the Dutch school in the pigment and brushwork of the face, and the painting of the flesh is very smooth and shiny. After 1700—and we are told that about this time he was much influenced by Rubens—we see a change. From that time onwards the greater number of his pictures are of rougher brushwork and the colours more boldly handled; whilst in the last ten years there is the natural decline of an older and failing man. To my mind, as soon as Kneller arrived in England he saw the works of Lely, and realized in what direction a good market lay. His classical training, especially the time he had spent in copying the works of masters both in Italy and Hamburg, made it easy for him to adapt and modify his work to the demand of the English public. The change in his work towards the end of the century was a change that arose from the natural trend of fashion and taste. The Restoration had demanded a coarseness and vulgarity which had been in part counteracted during the reign of William and Mary. Now, at the end of their reign, the further reaction which led to the age of taste in the eighteenth century had begun.

Kneller had studied to be a historical painter as well as a portrait painter, but quickly realized that a great future lay in the latter branch of the artist's profession. He remarked on one occasion, as Haydon was to find to his cost:

'History painters paint history and don't begin to live until they are dead. I paint the living. They make me live.'

Kneller painted the living—in fact, he painted every eminent person of his day, and his canvases are in many cases all that remain to tell us of the character and appearance of his contemporaries. Though not depicting heroic scenes, he really painted more historical figures than any other man: a glance through the catalogue in Appendix B or D 1 will suffice to show this.

When Kneller came to England first, Lely, who had followed Van Dyck, was supreme. Lely had lived through a hard period. He began in the reign of Charles I, had to struggle through the dismal Commonwealth period, and then was caught in the full flood of the excesses of the Restoration. When Kneller arrived the first exuberance of the Restoration had died down. A glance at a Lely woman and a Kneller woman will quickly show this. The Lely will show a grosser though a more gaily dressed woman, perhaps with the breast bared, whilst Kneller will show a graceful but formal lady most correctly dressed. His only excess would be that the woman might be represented allegorically as a saint or goddess, for it was not until the next century that women were again painted as themselves instead of being made to represent some allegorical figure not always in conformity with their character.

That Kneller could draw and paint well there is no doubt. One need only look at any of the pictures mentioned in the catalogue in Appendix B, which includes works that are certainly by Godfrey Kneller himself, for this to be proved. We are genuinely shocked when looking at his lesser works to find so many badly drawn and painted. What is the reason?

Kneller, first of all, lived in a day before the photographer. He had to replace the photographer. It is in this respect that we must pay some little attention. As a photographer he was commissioned to paint the men and women of his time; he was the fashionable painter and therefore everyone flocked to him. As happens with fashions, the judgment of the individual disappears; it was more important to be painted by the great Sir Godfrey than to have a well-painted portrait. The studio trade-mark was one thing that mattered. If he did not paint all the commissions he received, he would not only lose much money but would rapidly go out of fashion. The result was that he accepted them all, and having accepted more than he could paint, it was natural that the work should be hurried and slipshod, whilst more and more passed to the hands of assistants. Like a photographer, so many copies were often required, and this fact increased the number of bad pictures.

There are many references and accounts by contemporaries who sat to Kneller, and from their accounts it is easy to see how his system worked.

First of all it was necessary to make an appointment, which had to be done some time ahead; even the monarchs often made their way to his studio at Covent Garden or Great Queen Street. The subject would then be shown into the studio, where, if an important person, Godfrey Kneller would pose them and sketch in

43. CRUCIFIXION (1686)

Lord Fairhaven, Anglesey Abbey

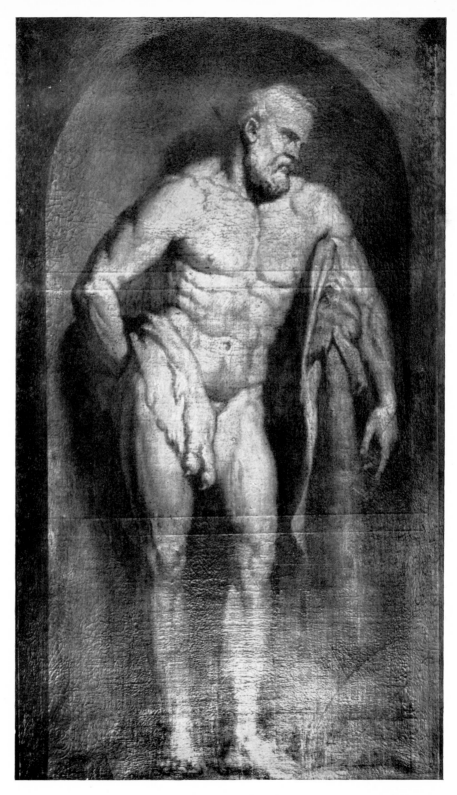

44. HERCULES (1716)

the *pentimento*. He might make a sketch in ink such as the *Design for a Fancy Portrait* in the Victoria and Albert Museum (39). If not such an important person, then perhaps Gaspar, who had done the same for Lely, would pose the subject and sketch in the pose before summoning Godfrey, who would then paint in the head and hands. A picture almost in this state can be seen in the Kit Kat collection: that of Viscount Shannon shows just the head and *pentimento* (78). After Godfrey had finished these, which he would do in an hour or two whilst surrounded by his friends and friends of the sitters all paying him the greatest compliments, the background and clothing had to be done. Again, if it was an important personage this would be done by Kneller, but more often than not, a model would replace the actual sitter and the dress and background would be painted in or finished by the studio hands. This accounts for the same dress and coat being worn by different people. The whole work would be finished in a day or two and then the sitter would be summoned to see if he liked it, for Godfrey did not like adverse criticisms, as is shown, for example, by this letter from Samuel Pepys to Kneller on 24th March 1702:

'For God's sake, my old friend, look once more over my letter of yesterday, and tell me what one word is in it that should occasion any syllable of what your man brings from you this morning.'

After the picture had been finally approved a number of copies might be ordered; sometimes these would be of different size from the original, and would be dispatched to relations, friends or institutions. The copies made in the studio would perhaps be supervised by Kneller, who again might even paint in the hands and face, but more often than not they would be left to the studio hands to complete. Others would take their picture away and have it copied by a local artist; thus accounting for the frequent repetitions of the same picture in the same area.

As a special concession, when Alexander Pope commissioned Godfrey in his later years to paint Lady Wortley Montagu, Kneller went to the subject's house and took a drawing of the head in pencil or crayon, and that was the only time he saw his sitter.

Kneller's prices went up a little towards the end of his life, but from the study of contemporary receipts they appear fairly constant, perhaps fluctuating either way by a pound or two. They were on an average fifteen guineas for a head, twenty if one hand was shown, thirty for a half-length and sixty for a whole-length. To obtain present-day values these sums should be multiplied by about six. The average price in a sale-room, unless the picture is extraordinarily good or of some historic personage, is now under £100.

On account of a method of work which was caused by demand, it is obvious that many bad pictures would inevitably find their way on to the market, but Kneller did paint many good pictures which are in the best and highest tradition of portrait painting.

He was once asked by a tailor to take on his son as an apprentice, but the tailor was rebuffed by being told that this was an impossibility, and that only God could make a painter. This story has been frequently told as an example of Kneller's vanity—proving that he thought himself a specially chosen man. I feel this is unfair, for surely Kneller really meant that one must have a vocation to be an artist, whereas tailoring was a craft any man could be taught. Given that vocation to the art, Kneller was one of the first to admit that a long and classical training was necessary, and this training shows itself in all his best work.

In England he even went so far as to open an Academy of Painting in the year 1711. Though this Academy did not last very long, since Kneller fought with most of those who assisted in it, it proves that he had a desire to further good painting and was not solely occupied with his own fortunes.

Kneller's position in the history and development of English painting is important owing to the fact that he was the last of the foreign school, and directly through him, especially on account of his Academy, arose the great English portrait painters beginning with Hogarth and Reynolds, passing on to Romney and Gainsborough through the nineteenth century until we arrive at the age of Orpen, Lavery and John.

When Kneller was painting, the landscape artist was almost unheard of, though Rubens mastered the art, and it was only at the beginning of the eighteenth century that this new style of painter was appearing in France. During Kneller's lifetime, the only landscape painting was that which filled in the back of a canvas behind a figure—it might be an allegorical background, a battle or perhaps a house or castle. The only professional artists other than the portrait painters were the history painters. They too specialized first of all in the figure, whilst the setting of the historical scene, whether it represented legend or contemporary history, was secondary to the personages. Towards the end of Kneller's life, the landscape painters who made the figures subservient to nature began to work.

Since the age of Holbein, portrait painting, especially that of the wealthy for the adornment of their own halls, until Kneller's time was dominated by foreigners; of whom Van Dyck, Lely and Kneller are the best known. It cannot be denied that when these painters during the seventeenth century worked at their best they reached the standard of the greatest masters; and there is a tendency to say that painting declined as each of these foreign masters succeeded the other. I do not think that the actual technique or the painters declined, but certainly taste and judgment altered, and when Kneller was painting the mediocre was accepted, with the result that artists did not give of their best all the while. Kneller at his height was as fine a draughtsman and colourist as Van Dyck, and to my mind nearly always superior to Lely, but at his worst his slap-dash work was beneath contempt. It is possible to select twelve portraits by Kneller, and if the selection is judicious, the student might well place him at the top of the tree of portrait painting, or if bad, reckon him among the worst of local or family artists. On account of this unevenness Kneller's reputation has suffered.

Kneller arrived in England when it was the fashion to have foreign portrait

45. WRIOTHESLEY, LORD RUSSELL (1686)

Engraved by J. Beckett, after picture at Woburn

46. LORD BUCKHURST AND LADY MARY SACKVILLE

Lord Sackville, Knole

painters in the same way that to-day head waiters are French, and ice-cream merchants Italian. It was a vogue which resulted in many good native artists both from England and Ireland being pushed into oblivion and forgotten. He arrived at the right moment, for he was the last foreign master to dominate English portraiture.

In Appendix B, I have given a list of pictures by Kneller which may be of some interest to the student who wishes to make a more detailed study. There is one great difficulty which confronts any person making a study of Kneller—and that is to decide what is by the master himself; what is from his studio and chiefly the work of his assistants; and lastly what is merely after him. His painting influenced all other contemporary painters, for they imitated him to follow the fashion.

In identifying pictures a signature is naturally the first thing for which one looks, and a good number of pictures by him were signed. His usual method of signature was either with his initials G. K. or his name in full—Kneller—in both cases the G. usually ran into the K. After his being knighted in 1692 he would add the word 'Eques' and possibly write in 'fecit'; but he appears to have had no rule and though his method of signature differs frequently, he did not even adopt one particular method at one particular period. The dating of the work appears optional.

Then there are many fine paintings which show the pencil and brush of the master which bear neither signature nor date, whilst there are others which one blushes to note are signed and dated. One must, however, accept those which are signed and dated other than obvious frauds. There has never been a financial demand for his work, therefore frauds are rare. Others which are well drawn and painted one can also attribute to his hand. But the many studio or 'after' pictures are difficult to place in the correct category. It seems to me best that we accept those which have his definite characteristics, for if he did not himself lay the paint on, at least we are certain that he influenced the work in every way. We are therefore, on this basis, able to consider as works of Kneller all those by him, from his studio, or after him, which were painted during his lifetime. But in many a country house I have seen labels affixed to pictures claiming Kneller as the painter, and more often than not these are the works of Dahl, Wissing, Wright, Jervas and others whom the labeller did not know. Frequently I have found such labels stuck on by members of the family on hearsay when a glance at the clothing or coiffure will prove that the painting was not done within ten or fifteen years of Kneller's lifetime.

There are certain characteristics which a short study will rapidly show. First of all, as I have said, Kneller drew well, and usually his face and hands are excellently drawn, though he was in the habit of lengthening the oval of the face. In the original picture it is often possible to see where the painter has worked around the edge and shape of the face, whilst the copies, which were often traced, show a far firmer paint line and less search for shape. At his best the eyes and nose were finely drawn, and as far as men were concerned he did not necessarily flatter. In many works there is the beginning of that realism which later showed itself in Hogarth, Highmore and Richardson. He was handicapped by painting in an era when men wore wigs which were getting ever longer and more ornate, and women's coiffures were growing more and more fantastic. Kneller would frequently take the wig off, showing his subject either in his own hair, as in the excellent *William Wycherley* (5) at Knole, or in a turban, as in the *Duke of Grafton* (34) or *Tonson* in the Kit Kat Club (77). This gave an opportunity of further study of the face. His wigs were of the simplest, and a close study of the corkscrew curls show the thinnest of paint squiggles which yet give the effect. As I have pointed out, until the turn of the century his faces were very smooth, after the Dutch tradition, but he never used the excessively vivid and shiny colours which distinguish the works of Michael Dahl. They can be well compared at the National Maritime Museum at Greenwich. His men's clothes too he often simplified to such an extent that the severe critic notes that the type of material was not distinguishable. Rather than paint his women in the ornate coiffure of the day he cut down their headwear considerably, which greatly added to their character and created dissimilarities. This is well shown in his later pictures such as the *Sarah, Duchess of Marlborough* at Blenheim or *The Countess of Mar* at Alloa (2). The *Hampton Court Beauties* were painted before the coiffure reached its height of absurdity. Fine examples of his women are *Mrs. Cross*, engraved by an unknown artist (48), and *The Countess of Sunderland* in the National Portrait Gallery (49).

Some writers, especially during the past fifty years, have abused the works of Kneller, so that except in the case of portraits of exceptional historical interest his present-day value in pounds is often less than the original cost in pounds in far higher value. This was not only due to his many bad pictures but also to fashion. His pictures were dismissed as all of one stamp. This is an easy generalization when merely glancing at his bewigged men—but is quite untrue the moment careful study begins.

Look at his pictures, say, of the writers—Congreve in the Senate Room at Trinity College, Dublin; Dryden at Trinity, Cambridge (3); Steele in the Kit Kat collection (47); and Pope (72). Congreve and Steele are painted in wigs, and each gives a particularly fine character study. There is the witty Congreve, the intellectual Dryden, the humorous Steele and the bitter Pope. His portraits of Evelyn at the Royal Society (11), of Pepys at Magdalene, Cambridge, and Greenwich (10), tell, in the clear and simple strokes of the brush, as much of their character as one obtains in reading their diaries. There is in these works an effort to probe deeper than the mere visual aspect of the sitter as Lely and Van Dyck had done, and we start to see the attempt to show more than just the mere outline and colour of the sitter's face; we begin to perceive that effort to comprehend character at which Hogarth in the next generation became so proficient. Other portraits worthy of study include the *Rev. John Howe* (52) and *Albemarle* (54) in the National Portrait Gallery, and *Southwell* (53) at the Royal Society.

47. SIR RICHARD STEELE (1717)

National Portrait Gallery (Kit Kat Collection)

48. MRS. CROSS

Unknown Engraver

49. ANN, COUNTESS OF SUNDERLAND

50. ITALIAN GREYHOUND (1696)

(This dog was the property of Lord Albemarle, and blue velvet buckled collar
embroidered in gold ' KEPPEL,' is at Quidenham)

Sir Godfrey Thomas, St. James's Palace

In his painting of men Kneller excelled. I do not think that he reached the same height with his women. This may also have been due to the age. His women, though well and formally painted, are stiff and serious; he does not seem to have grasped their character in the same way. Perhaps this was due to his own rather coarse outlook, which was representative of the day. Many of his women are dull—deadly dull—despite their drawing and painting, and often bear out Pope's 'Most women have no character at all.' There are exceptions, suchas the portraits of *Anne Oldfield* (55) and *Jane Smyth* (56).

But what sympathy he lacked in his painting of women he made up for in his docility and tenderness in painting children. His portrait of Lord Buckhurst and his sister Lady Mary Sackville feeding the little deer at Knole is as charming and as happy a picture as can be found (46). The Duke of Bedford has another picture at Woburn which is equally charming of young Wriothesley Russell, later to be the 2nd Duke of Bedford (45).

Kneller painted a few other pictures which I must mention to show his varied skill. There is the small *Crucifixion* which Lord Fairhaven has at Anglesey Abbey, which, as I mentioned, shows Kneller as St. Peter. This is delightful, and when he painted it on its smooth panel he must have had his Dutch masters in mind. Sir Godfrey Thomas has a picture of a dog by Kneller which hangs in his apartment at St. James's Palace (50). Kneller also produced mural paintings and ceilings. He designed those murals which Laguerre executed for him at Whitton, and also designed a ceiling at Handsworth House. Both have now disappeared; the former have been painted out and the latter destroyed in the fire of 1797. George Saurat, writing of his travels in England in the reigns of George I and George II, mentions paintings by Kneller of the 'Apostle in the Dome of St. Paul's' above the altar, but of these I cannot trace any remains and I think they may have been done as a temporary work for his friend Wren. He painted Wren at least four times; there are portraits in the Bodleian, at the National Portrait Gallery, at the Royal Society (57) and in St. Paul's Deanery.

For Pope he painted three classical statues which are now at Cirencester. Their drawing is excellent (44).

No, Kneller as a painter, despite the disadvantages of his age, excelled as a master, and is the link between the foreign-dominated English school and the purely English.

If he had lived in another age, his name as an artist might not have been so absurd, and Vertue was only recording an historical fact when he wrote before Kneller's death: 'In England no work of distinction but what has pieces of his performance.'

CHAPTER VI

HIS CONTEMPORARY PAINTERS

WHEN Godfrey Kneller arrived in England in 1676 he found Sir Peter Lely installed as the supreme master. We have written of Lely's and Kneller's painting of Charles II, and it has been said that Lely died of chagrin at seeing himself being dispossessed of his unique position by the young Kneller, but this is untrue.

Lely had come to England in 1641, according to Vertue, and had just over-lapped Van Dyck, then an old man. When he had arrived he found that William Dobson, an English pupil of Van Dyck's, was his chief rival. Lely, a Westphalian who had been trained in the Dutch school, was quick to realize what was required of him. He had seen the type of picture which Van Dyck had created, he studied the development of English painting from the formal and characterless anonymous flat paintings of the Elizabethan period, followed by the gradual development in early Jacobean times of the foreigners Marc Gheeraerts, Paul Van Somer, Cornelius Janssen and Daniel Mytens. He had received a good classical training, and he knew both how to draw and how to apply colour: the result was his immediate success. His development was divided into periods—the first in the reign of Charles I when his early works show the traditions of Van Dyck; the middle period during the Commonwealth when Puritan austerity forbade him to use much colour in the clothes and dresses but made him concentrate on the character in the head; and finally the period of the Restoration, when he was able to let himself go.

It was during this period that Lely reached his peak of popularity. It was the time of the painting of the Windsor *Beauties*, now with Kneller's *Beauties* at Hampton Court. All women were painted as some mythical or allegorical char-acter, whilst the men's dash was exaggerated in every possible way. The baroque had come to England with the return of Charles II, and Lely had rapidly been able to absorb it.

Like Kneller, Lely painted too many pictures, but whilst I would consider the best of Kneller—such as the *Matthew Prior* at Cambridge (51) or *The Chinese Convert* at Kensington Palace—far exceeded Lely both in drawing and pigment, I must admit that Lely did not turn out so many bad pictures from his studio as Kneller.

During the seventeenth century the foreigner had predominated. The leading painters had been successively Peter Paul Rubens, Anthony Van Dyck and Peter Lely, besides the lesser men who follow in the wake of the great masters; Kneller was in the direct line of succession (as Appendix C shows). However, each of

51. MATTHEW PRIOR

Trinity College, Cambridge

52. REV. JOHN HOWE

53. ROBERT SOUTHWELL (1690)

54. THE 1ST EARL OF ALBEMARLE (*circa* 1690)

these foreign masters had a number of English assistants and pupils; thus George Jameson (1586-1644), known as the Van Dyck of Scotland, was a pupil of Rubens, whilst William Dobson was Van Dyck's pupil, and Mary Beale, John Riley and others Lely's.

We therefore find that though the masters are foreigners, all through the century there is a native school which is subject to their influence but in its own time developing to some extent on national lines besides influencing succeeding masters. The number of English artists increased, as did their reputation, all through the seventeenth century, until the time when, on Kneller's arrival, six out of twelve leading portrait painters were English. This development continued into the eighteenth century, when the English became the masters and the foreigners the mere assistants and copyists.

In Appendix C is a diagram showing exactly where Godfrey Kneller stands from an historical viewpoint in the development of painting from Elizabethan times up to the height of the English school under Reynolds and Gainsborough in the second half of the eighteenth century, to the decline which set in in the later years of George III and led to the days of Opie and Lawrence. In this chart I have shown the artists in chronological order from the year or approximate year of their birth. This is perhaps misleading, for the period which is important is that during which they were painting in England and many of those shown spent their early years abroad, whilst others went abroad when they could not make a living in England.

In 1676 the portrait painters of England were divided into three groups: first, the school of Lely, which consisted of Peter Lely and his three leading pupils, Mrs. Beale, John Greenhill and William Wissing; secondly, the rivals of Lely, who included British John Riley and Scottish Joseph Michael Wright, besides the foreigners Gerard Soest, John Hayles and Huysman. The third group consists of a miscellany of painters including Richard Gibson, a relic of Van Dyck days, and two visiting Frenchmen, Paul Mignard and Henry Gaspar, besides the Italian mural painter and decorator, Antonio Verrio, whom Charles II had brought over to design tapestries but who had been set to work to redecorate Windsor and later Hampton Court.

I have omitted to mention other painters such as Robert Streater, a Court painter who designed and painted the ceiling of the Sheldonian Theatre at Oxford, for although he did occasionally paint a portrait it was not his chief *métier*.

Mrs. Mary Beale (1632-1697) was one of the earliest English women artists. She came, like so many artists and contrary to popular belief, from a good family —her father was the minister at Walton, Bucks, a Mr. Craddock by name, and her mother was a gracious lady, as her bust proves. Walpole says she painted in the 'Italian' style, but this I cannot myself see. I do notice, however, a very strong Dutch influence which might well be expected to have passed to her through her master. Owing to her early upbringing in a minister's household she found herself largely employed in painting clerical gentlemen and prelates—nearly every episcopal palace holds work by Mary Beale, and there are, of course, a large number in the Oxford Colleges. There is a strong tendency for dead-brownish colours to creep into her work. This gives an effect of half-tones and causes her pictures to be dull and without much light; some of her works are difficult to identify, for she liked to experiment both in her colours and her canvases. On the whole her paintings were very ordinary. I would cite as typical examples of her good work those of *Charles II* and *Cowley* in the National Portrait Gallery; the *Colonel Lovelace* at Dulwich and the *Unknown Youth* at Hardwick. Her son, Charles Beale, was also a portrait painter of some note who flourished until the arrival of William III. There is a portrait by him in the Fitzwilliam.

Lely's most promising pupil, John Greenhill, died just as Godfrey Kneller arrived in England. His father was Registrar at Salisbury Cathedral and Greenhill was born there in 1649. He came to London and entered the Lely studio. Unfortunately—and I have noticed it in others brought up within the precincts of cathedrals—he lived a rather too excessive life as far as drink was concerned. One day in 1676, when he was only twenty-seven, he was returning very drunk from a visit to the Vine Tavern, when he appears to have fallen into the gutter in Long Acre, where he was discovered unconscious and taken off to the house of Parry Walton, another painter, and there he died. His death may have been a loss to English painting. He was still in the hands of his master, and he painted so like Lely at this period that it is impossible to differentiate between their work at first sight. His drawing and painting were excellent, and it may well be that had he not died so young he might have become a formidable rival to Kneller. As it was he left us few pictures, but these are of real interest—for example, the *Baptist May* at Petworth, which may well be compared with the portrait of the same subject by Lely at Kensington; the *James Duke of York* at Dulwich; and the *Lord Shaftesbury* in the National Portrait Gallery.

William Wissing, the third of Lely's eminent pupils, was the youngest; unlike Mary Beale and John Greenhill he was a foreigner born at Amsterdam, and like Greenhill he died young—at the age of thirty-one in 1687. When Kneller arrived he was only twenty, and it is said that he originally came over from Holland as a footman to Peter Lely but was found copying his master's work. Lely was pleased and encouraged him, and after Lely's death in 1680 he had a considerable success for a few years, especially in the painting of women, such as the *Mrs. Lawson* and *Mrs. Knott* at Hampton Court or the *Maria D'Este* in the National Portrait Gallery. The poses are those of Lely but the drawing is inferior and the painting very washy—in fact, the paint is so thin and light that his rather commonplace portraits, especially of women, of which he produced many in his short seven years of fame, are easily recognizable.

I shall discuss in chronological order the rivals of Lely who were painting in 1676 and were therefore those with whom Godfrey Kneller was destined to compete. The eldest was Joseph Michael Wright, born about 1625 in Scotland;

in 1671 we find him signing himself 'Pictor Regis,' so that we safely infer that when Kneller arrived he was an established portrait painter. The earliest known work of Wright's is the portrait of Cromwell's daughter Elizabeth Claypole which hangs in the National Portrait Gallery. His early work shows a strong influence of Van Dyck, but we do not know who his master was—in fact, I think he may well have been self-taught.

At quite an early age he came to London and was employed on two series of pictures of the *Judges*, the first about 1640 and the second some twenty years later, which now hang in the London Guildhall. His work has individuality and colouring and drawing rather distinctive to him. His faces are usually narrow and his eyes set wide apart; the paint is very thinly applied and, in contrast with Mary Beale, his pictures are bright and full of high lights. We have it from Vertue that he used a great deal of medium, including varnish mixed up with his paint. His dresses were full of detail, and although with more shape and light, as pernickety at times as those of the typical Elizabethan artist.

He was a considerable rival to Lely, to whom he really took second place. In fact, Lely had previously been asked to paint the *Judges* but could not do so; the natural second choice then was Wright. Michael Wright did not confine his interests to painting; he was a friend of Roger Palmer, Lord Castlemaine, and in 1686 accompanied him on a diplomatic mission to Rome, returning in 1688. On his return he found that Kneller had taken all his practice and he was unable now to obtain a commission; the next few years were lean for him, and whilst he had been able to compete with Lely he was now unable to compete with the young Kneller. In 1700 Wright applied to King William for the post of King's Painter in Scotland, but according to him a 'shop keeper was preferred.'

Michael Wright's pictures are very consistent and if he had concentrated on painting he might have been a greater master than Lely. There is an interesting picture at Hampton Court and a copy in the Garrick Club of John Lacy the comedian in three different rôles—as Parson Scruple in *Cheats*, Sly in *The Taming of the Shrew*, and Monsieur de Vice in *The Country Captain*. Walpole says that this picture was painted in 1675, but Collins Baker, I think rightly, attributes it to an earlier date. In the National Portrait Gallery there are three good portraits—*Thomas Hobbes*, *Matthew Hale* and *Charles II*; and at Oxford we find an interesting *Bishop of Winchester* at Christ Church and *Prince Rupert* at Magdalen. Wright died in 1700 in London and for the last twenty-five years had found himself, as I have explained, outpaced by the young Kneller.

A contemporary and equal rival to Lely and to Wright was Gerard Soest; though some twelve years younger than Wright, he came to England at an early age, certainly some time before the Restoration. Soest, like Lely, was born in Westphalia, in about 1637 or perhaps a little earlier. That on his arrival in England he was immediately influenced by Van Dyck is clearly discernible in his early works. As he succeeded, so he found himself, like all others, having to compete with Lely. In comparison with both Lely and Wright, his heads were drawn and painted in bold relief, appeared very animated and were highly finished. His clothes are noticeable for their bright colours, especially when he was painting women's dresses, although the pigment of the face and hands did not show Lely's dexterity, but more often than not, in his male portraits, the heads showed more character and individuality than Lely's. We know of a good head of *John Wallis* (of the famous correspondence with Kneller, see p. 65) by him in the Royal Society, besides the *Colonel Blood* in the National Portrait Gallery, the series in oval of the six sons of Sir Thomas Lyttelton at Hagley, *Miss Harley* at Welbeck and *Fuller, Bishop of Lincoln*, at Christ Church.

Gerard Soest died in 1681, some five years after Kneller arrived in England, at the age of forty-five or thereabouts; he therefore died in his prime and did not live to be his rival, but his influence passed to his chief pupil John Riley, who was born in London in the same year as Kneller, and when the latter arrived in London they were both aged thirty and entering their peak as painters.

Horace Walpole has described John Riley as 'one of the best painters that has flourished in England, whose talents whilst living were obscured by the fame rather than the merit of Kneller, and depressed since by being confounded with Lely, an honour unlucky to his reputation.'

This praise is perhaps a little lavish. Riley began his studies under Isaac Fuller, but shortly afterwards transferred himself to the school of Soest. He was rather eclipsed until the death of Lely and Soest, when he became a popular painter; but though a serious rival at the time to Kneller, there is no doubt to my mind which was the greater master. Walpole is right in that many of his early works closely resemble Lely, but his drawing is not so firm.

In character Riley, 'a gentleman,' according to Vertue, 'extremely courteous in his behaviour, engaging in his conversation and prudent in all his actions,' is an interesting contrast to Kneller's, for it would be hard to find a more humble person. Contemporary records say that he was very diffident about his own works and often disgusted at them. When he was painting he disliked anyone watching him—how unlike Godfrey painting whilst all the wits flattered him! Once Riley had completed a picture, then his sitters and patrons could criticize to their heart's content, and the amiable painter would make alterations according to their views. This may well account for the uneven standard of his work, but occasionally he manages to obtain definite character in his sitters, such as the *Lord William Russell* of the National Portrait Gallery.

Like Kneller he painted many monarchs, and his work did not flatter Charles II, who, on seeing his picture by Riley, said: 'Is this like me? Then odds fish, I am an ugly fellow.'

His early pictures are in the style of Lely, but between 1685 until the year of his death in 1691 the influence of Kneller is noticeable, though throughout he makes great use of carmine in lining the face; we may note that this was also a trick of Soest. He painted very few women, but the National Portrait Gallery

55. ANNE OLDFIELD (1702)

The Garrick Club

56. LADY JANE SMYTH (1713)

Nottingham City Art Gallery

contains many examples of his work, including a picture of Dr. Burnett and another of Edmund Waller.

To my mind Riley was rightly eclipsed by Kneller, and this eclipse was due to Kneller's superiority in composition, colour and drawing, not because of the vogue for a foreigner or on account of drive and push.

This brief biographical review of Lely's rivals, who became Kneller's on his arrival, must also include mention of John Hayles and James Huysman. Hayles died three years after Kneller's arrival in England, but Huysman lived to vie with him for twenty years.

Readers of Samuel Pepys's *Diary* will know the name of Hayles, for he was a friend of Pepys and is frequently mentioned between 1666 and 1668. A Dutchman, born very early in the century, Hayles came to England some time before the Restoration. He was a very inferior rival to Lely, but, unlike Lely, had been trained in his native school under Miereveldt. His faces are usually rather large and over life-size, whilst the poses are hard and uncomfortable. There is nothing English about Hayles's work, and, unlike so many foreigners who came over, he never seems to have acclimatized his painting or modified it to the more delicate English genre. There is a picture of his friend Pepys in the National Portrait Gallery; besides good portraits his best work is of Lady Anne and Lady Diana Russell at Woburn. He died in London in 1677.

According to Walpole, James Huysman was born in 1656, but this is definitely incorrect. Mr. Collins Baker in his *Lely and the Stuart Portrait Painters* goes into the year of Huysman's birth in great detail, coming to the conclusion that it was about 1633, a year we can accept. Had he been born in 1656, when Godfrey arrived he would only have been twenty, whilst we know that he was already an established painter and rival to Lely. Huysman (or Housman as he is sometimes called) was born in Amsterdam and was a pupil of Bakerel, who Vertue says 'was brought up with Van Dyck in the School of Rubens.' Huysman when he came to England during Charles II's reign reintroduced some 'Rubens' and 'Van Dyck' blood. Huysman is interesting, for although he arrived as a history painter he became a portrait painter and eventually specialized in women and children. It is noticeable in the review of portrait painters to date, that little mention has been made of the paintings of women. The seventeenth-century painters, certainly up to the third quarter, were not successful with their women subjects—chiefly on account of the hardness of design and the baroque tastes of the period; only Lely alone had really painted women on any scale.

Huysman's work is noticeable for the rough and solid painting, and his women are unmistakable owing to his habit of giving them thin and tapering hands. There is a child portrait of Anne's son, William, Duke of Gloucester, at Kensington Palace which is very pleasing and attractive. Also at Hampton Court there are full-lengths of Catherine of Braganza and Lady Byron which Vertue says 'did some great service'; of his male pictures the best known on account of

I

its frequent reproduction is his *Izaak Walton* in the National Portrait Gallery. Huysman died in London in 1696.

Before going into detail as to the painters who arrived in England or matured during Kneller's life in this country, I must just make mention of four others: Richard Gibson (1616-1690), Paul Mignard (1639-1691), Henry Gaspar (1625-1701) and Antonio Verrio (1639-1707).

Gibson is remarkable as a curiosity rather than as a painter. He was a dwarf who was page to a lady at Mortlake, liked painting and became a pupil of Francesco Cleyn, and although not a pupil or student of Lely he became a copyist of this painter. He married a dwarf, each of them being only three feet ten inches high. There was a picture of Lely with this diminutive pair, but I cannot now trace its whereabouts. Born in Cumberland, Gibson later became a page to Henrietta Maria and subsequently taught both Princess Mary of Orange and her sister Anne to draw. Of his nine children five grew up to normal size, the family producing quite a long line of mediocre painters. Although so far as can be traced he did no original work, as a copyist and draughtsman he was a figure, though rather a small one, in the painting world. Mignard and Gaspar were both French, and introduced a French influence into English painting which during Kneller's life was to be developed by Nicholas Largillière. Mignard was born at Avignon and was a nephew of the eminent French painter Pierre Mignard. Not much is now known of his work here except that he painted a picture of Lady Meath which is at Kilruddery, County Wicklow, and also the Ladies Anne and Henrietta Churchill at Blenheim. He returned to France to die there. He may well have come over, as did Henry Gaspar, in the train of Louise de Kerouaille, Duchess of Portsmouth. Gaspar came to London in 1670, but returned to France with his patroness in 1685.

Of Gaspar's work, which is noticeable for its lightness and delicacy if not for its vigour, we know more. At Wilton there is a picture of Philip, Earl of Pembroke, who married the Duchess of Portsmouth's sister; at Hagley Hall is Lord Cobham's picture of the Duchess of Portsmouth. Gaspar and Mignard were both painting and much in favour when Kneller arrived.

Antonio Verrio was brought over by Charles II to design some tapestries, but instead became the leading mural artist and decorator of the day. This involved the painting of portraits from models, and more often than not he inserted his friends into his mythological or allegorical works. At St. George's Hall, Windsor, for instance, was the mural painting already mentioned depicting Christ healing the sick; among the spectators could be discerned portraits of Godfrey Kneller and Baptist May in long periwigs, but only the head of William III remains.

If we remember that the foreigners Lely and Wissing, and the native painters Beale, Wright and Riley, were the leading portrait painters when Godfrey Kneller arrived, it will facilitate our tracing the development of rivals after his appearance in England. As in previous years, so during his life here the portrait painters can be divided into foreign masters and native craftsmen. The foreign masters came over once they had become proficient in their art, whilst the native painters studied from the foreigners, and may well have travelled abroad to increase their efficiency. There was one change, however, during this period of fifty years when portrait painting suffered through the unsettled period; during the reign of William and Mary we begin to see the rise of the native artist to the rank of master, whilst the foreigners became the assistants. During this period again, as we shall see, the English school was responsible for influencing the development of painting not only in Scotland and Ireland but also in France and America. As we review the list of painters who arrived or developed at this time we at once notice that whilst the foreigners except Kneller are mainly forgotten, the Englishmen's names are still remembered by the most superficial of amateurs of portrait painting.

Around the year 1780 Michael Dahl arrived from Sweden, Nicholas Largillière from France and Godfrey Schalken from Hanover; whilst in the succeeding five years there came John Closterman, also from Hanover; Louis Laguerre, like Largillière, from France; and John Medina from Spain via Antwerp.

The native painters who developed and began to work during Godfrey's life in England included Jonathan Richardson, Charles Jervas, Sir James Thornhill, John Smibert, Joseph Highmore and William Hogarth.

Michael Dahl was to be Kneller's chief contemporary rival and was to hold the stage as the last of the Stuart painters for twenty years after Kneller's death. Although he came to England at the age of twenty-three, about 1680, he left again in 1682 to travel to Rome and returned in about 1688. By then Godfrey Kneller was well established, but Michael Dahl managed to compete well against him. Although there was the report in Vertue of Kneller no longer patronizing the enameller Zinke because he had spoken well of Dahl, it would appear that, at any rate at first, the two got on well together, for Kneller painted Dahl's portrait, and Michael Dahl contributed many pictures towards the series of Greenwich *Admirals*. Greenwich gives us an easy and ready means of seeing similar subjects by Kneller and Dahl hung side by side. One at once notices that Michael Dahl's pigment is far smoother and thinner than Kneller's, and with the exception of the *Sir Cloudesley Shovell*, there is not the same character in the faces of his Admirals. On the other hand, his pictures would appear better finished. The wigs and clothing are worked in detail, often with the point of the brush, instead of the mere impression of cloth and ornament which Kneller often gives. Walpole wrote that Dahl 'did not neglect anything except the head like Godfrey Kneller, and drew the rest of the figure much better than Richardson.' This may have been true, but Dahl did not reach the same mastery as Kneller and his works remain as decorative and efficient portraits lacking in character and inspiration. Dahl's women, who are often more beautiful than Kneller's, may be seen at Petworth, where there are six known as *The Petworth Beauties*. His thin and fluent paint is more appropriate for women than for men, but the effect is more like a modern advertisement for some cold cream than a series of studies of interesting women.

Nicholas Largillière is of interest in that he came to England bringing with him the delicacy of the French school, as may be seen in his *Mrs. Middleton* in the National Portrait Gallery; but not being in sympathy with the Revolution of 1689 he left again to return to France. Here he rapidly became acclaimed as the French Van Dyck, but studying the many excellent portraits by him in the Louvre, such as that of *Charles le Brun* which gave him entry into the French Academy or the *Self-portrait* at Versailles, one can see the influence of the English school of the Stuarts. His great success in France was in fact largely due to his training in England. He came over just before Lely's death to assist him as an apprentice, which entailed a visit to Windsor to repair a picture. Here he met Charles II, who took a great liking to the boy and commissioned him to paint. Later he maintained this connection with the family, and there now hang in the National Portrait Gallery two attractive pictures of *Cardinal York* and *The Young Pretender* as children.

Of Godfrey Schalken we know little except that he either had a little talent or great influence, for he made his way into the Court, painted William III by candlelight—showing William himself holding a candle; later he repeated this work, this time inserting his own head. Little else is known of him and our only informants are Vertue and Walpole; he can therefore be dismissed as no serious rival to Godfrey, and no real influence on the English school, though Vertue says his pictures were constantly increasing in value.

John Closterman arrived in England at the age of twenty-five in 1681. He was employed by Riley to paint draperies, but gradually found himself doing more of the picture, so that when Riley died in 1691, Closterman slipped readily into the vacancy created by his death. He painted a picture of Grinling Gibbons which according to Walpole was so successful that it 'set him in competition with Sir Godfrey Kneller.' Collins Baker refers to Closterman as the 'ultimate degradation of the Lelyesque,' and that is not an unfair criticism. If Dahl was the last of the Stuart painters, with Closterman died out the last of the Restoration influence, although at times he painted successful portraits such as that of *John Locke* after Kneller in the Portrait Gallery, the fine *Duke of Rutland* at Hardwick and a *Lord Granby* at Belvoir.

Louis Laguerre expected to be the natural successor to Verrio, but found himself thwarted at every turn as a mural painter by the native-born James Thornhill. I have included him, for, like Verrio, his work necessitated the painting of figures from life, and like Verrio and Thornhill he made use of actual people for this purpose. He was a Director of Godfrey Kneller's Academy in Great Queen Street, and in 1717, when Kneller resigned, Laguerre expected to succeed him, but found himself thwarted by Thornhill when the Academy was reopened again in 1724. At the same time he expected, and in fact it was arranged, that he should decorate the rebuilt St. Paul's, but it was Thornhill who did it; it was only

St Christopher Wren Kt.
President of the Royal
Society

57. SIR CHRISTOPHER WREN (1687)
(also attributed to Closterman-Riley)

The Royal Society

at Kneller's house at Whitton that Laguerre ousted Thornhill. As already stated, when Godfrey was redecorating his house there he had engaged Thornhill to decorate the stairs; just after he had been commissioned, Godfrey heard casually that Thornhill had painted some portraits. Laguerre was then commissioned to do the work, one of his masterpieces (Vertue) of which there is no trace left. There are some *Labours of Hercules* at Hampton Court, where he had discovered Mantegna's cartoons 'to the great satisfaction of the King and also the curious.' He painted most of the 'Verrio' decorations at St. Bartholomew's Hospital.

Thornhill himself had been born at Weymouth. He painted the dome of St. Paul's among other works; also historical scenes depicting the history of Queen Anne at Hampton Court, and became President of the revived Academy in 1724, where Hogarth studied and met Thornhill's daughter whom he married. Thornhill ousted the foreigner at decorating, as Hogarth was to oust the foreigner on portraits. But we are discussing the native Thornhill without mention of Sir John Baptist Medina. Medina was of Spanish origin though his father had settled in Antwerp. He came to England in 1686, to find that as far as London was concerned Kneller held sway, whilst to compete even with Dahl was beyond his power. So after studying the fashions of Court portrait painting he made his way to Edinburgh, taking to Scotland the mode of the Continent as modified by what he saw in London. He cannot be claimed as a great painter, but he practised in Edinburgh with great success, was the last Knight made before the Union, and is represented in the great Scottish private collections as well as by the portraits in the Surgeons' Hall. He died in Edinburgh in 1711.

Jonathan Richardson became a disciple of Riley's in 1687, and although strongly influenced by his master he did not achieve the close relationship with his master that Closterman had. However, though never of the same standard as Kneller, he painted many of the same subjects, such as Pope, Prior and Steele, and there is a portrait by him at Welbeck of *Abigail Harley*. Through Riley, Richardson became the first of the transitional portrait painters of the beginning of the eighteenth century. Richardson neither had the opportunity of painting in the Stuart days, nor lived long enough to benefit by the good taste of the next era. His drawing was not perfect and his painting hard and metallic; he was to become Highmore's master.

Charles Jervas, unlike any other portrait painter before him, was an Irishman. He was born at Clonliske near Shinrone in King's County about the same time that Kneller arrived in England. His father was John Jervas of Clonliske and his mother Elizabeth Baldwin of Shinrone. He was one of five brothers, and as he showed a definite taste for painting his family allowed him to proceed to London towards the end of the seventeenth century. In London he found his way to Godfrey's studio, and though not an assistant in the real sense like those of whom I write in the next chapter, for about a year Jervas worked in the studio, helping and learning from the master. Jervas was a bad draughtsman but his pigments were usually clear and his characterization fair, whilst his drapery was efficient. Kneller made a good *bon mot* on Jervas when the latter was successful. Jervas the bad draughtsman bought a coach and six horses; 'Ach, mein Gott,' said Godfrey, 'if his horses draw no better than he does he will never get to his journey's end.' Many of his works can easily be mistaken for late Knellers.

Whilst in London Jervas was befriended by one Norris, then keeper of the King's pictures. He gave Jervas the free run of the galleries at Hampton Court, where he copied Raphael's Cartoons. Dr. George Clarke, who played such an important part in the foundation of the Oxford art collections, also patronized young Jervas by buying his early pictures and sending him off for a while to study in Paris and Rome. He had learnt one thing of vanity from Godfrey, for we read that after copying a picture by Titian he exclaimed—proud of his success: 'Poor little Tit., how he would stare!'

About 1709 he returned to England, and it was then that he set up as a society portrait painter in opposition to Sir Godfrey. In London he moved in much the same circle, for indeed it was a small one crowded with great intellectual figures, and like Kneller he claimed Addison, Gay, Arbuthnot and Warburton among his friends and sitters. He painted Swift twice, once in London in about 1706, and once in Dublin about 1716, for he returned to Dublin to reintroduce into that country the taste for English portraiture which had first come in with the conquering army of William III. He later returned to England, where he instructed Pope in painting.

As a result of Jervas's influence in Ireland, we are able to trace the development of Irish portrait painting which began with Joseph Michael Wright (a nephew of the earlier English painter), Thomas Pooley, Francis Bindon and James Latham, and eventually led through Hussey, Hone and Hunter, Archer, Shee, Catterson Smith, to Shannon, Orpen and Lavery.

On Kneller's death in 1723 Jervas was appointed Royal Painter to George I, a position he also held under George II.

Jervas, born in Ireland, returned there for a short while to influence the fashions. John Smibert was born about 1684 in Edinburgh but did not return to his native country, instead taking the tradition of English portraiture to America. He had come to London, where he originally worked as a coach decorator, in about 1711 and entered Kneller's Academy in Great Queen Street; later, when Thornhill reopened the Academy, Smibert continued his studies under Thornhill. From the Academy he managed to travel abroad, like other painters copying the classical pictures and statues in Italy. On his return he met George Berkeley, Bishop of Cloyne, Swift's friend. Berkeley was interested in the inauguration of a College of Arts and Science in Bermuda. This was in 1726-27. The King had given his patronage to this scheme, and Smibert was chosen to go to Bermuda as a Professor. Whilst he was sailing across the Atlantic George I died and the project was dropped. Smibert was undaunted, for he had already overcome many difficulties since he was a house painter in Edinburgh, and proceeded to the continent of America, settling at Boston in New England, where he married and died; one of his sons, Nathaniel, became an artist in America, but it was Smibert who introduced traditional portraiture to that country. At Yale University there is a very large group by Smibert called *Dean Berkeley and his Entourage*; it is signed and dated 1729, and must have been painted after his arrival in America from the many sketches he did of his patron. This group is a fine example of the transition from Stuart to Georgian painting. The women remind one of Kneller, but the men begin to approach those of Hogarth and Hudson. In addition to painting original portraits, Smibert copied and recopied the masterpieces he had seen during his continental tour, thus introducing not only British portraiture but also the Renaissance to the new continent. His portrait of Berkeley is in the National Portrait Gallery, and there is another Berkeley group in Dublin.

Joseph Highmore, who first studied under Kneller and then under Richardson, was well established at the time of Kneller's death in 1723, but cannot be considered as a rival, for during the last four years of his life Godfrey painted little. Highmore was just older than Hogarth, but the younger painter greatly influenced Highmore, as can be seen in the set of illustrations for Richardson's *Pamela* which used to hang in the National Gallery and was broken up a few years ago, whilst there is a Hogarthian picture of Samuel Richardson in the Portrait Gallery. Highmore had great sense of colour and decoration though his perspective was often weak.

At the time of Kneller's death Hogarth had established himself as an engraver, but it was not until a year later that he entered Thornhill's Academy and developed as the master of English character painting. Kneller's influence can still be traced in certain of Hogarth's works, such as the painting of the face and general design of the *Captain Coram* at the Foundling Hospital, but a glance at *The Shrimp Girl* in the National Gallery tells where Hogarth found his inspiration.

So we see that Kneller arrived here to be influenced by Lely and departed this world exercising direct influence on Hogarth.

This was a long span, from the Restoration to the Georgian period. It was not a period in which the painters received all the encouragement they might have done, but it was the period before the vogue of the landscape painters, when portrait painting was supreme. During this time Kneller held his own as superior to any other foreign or native painter and at the same time influenced all those who arrived in England from other countries, or who grew up in the country in an academic tradition. If there was a fault it was the lack of critical faculty in a public which loved to be flattered.

CHAPTER VII

THE ASSISTANTS AND PUPILS

In the previous chapter I reviewed all Godfrey Kneller's chief contemporaries, mentioning certain of his pupils such as Highmore and Jervas. Although it may appear more like a catalogue than a consecutive account, I plan to deal in this chapter with his assistants.

Godfrey Kneller's studio methods have been discussed. His assistants in some cases were artists of merit in their own particular field, and Godfrey Kneller was greatly indebted to them. Although he frequently allowed them to finish off his works in a rough-and-ready manner, without them he would never have been able to turn out the large quantity of paintings which established his name and fame prior to the turn of the century. Some may say that had he not had the assistants he might have painted fewer pictures of better quality. It is interesting to note that up to the beginning of the eighteenth century we know a good deal about the assistants, whilst later they appear to be eclipsed. I think this is largely due to the fact that after about 1705 backgrounds other than curtains of a neutral shade disappeared. There no longer appears any need for the flower painter or the architectural painter. At the same time clothes, especially of ladies, became less ornate, so that the assistant's importance decreased. During the last fifteen years we only hear of Edward and Robert Byng assisting Godfrey, whilst before 1700 we read of Jean Baptist Gaspar painting poses; John James Backer, Marcel Laroon and John Pieters painting draperies; Jean Baptiste Monnoyer painting flower backgrounds, and Henry Vergazon architectural and landscape scenes. Jacob Van der Roer also assisted, whilst John Zachary Kneller and one Fancatti were about the studio as copyists. James Worsdale also helped in the interim period before the Byng brothers.

Jean Baptist Gaspar was perhaps in the most interesting position of any assistant. He was himself a great expert and judge of painting and had painted postures for Lely and Riley before Kneller. He witnessed and assisted the pictorial transition from the Restoration to the Revolution.

The painting of the Restoration Court had been described as: 'a mob of shepherds and shepherdesses in flowing wiges and dress'd curls, ruffled Endymions, humble Junos, withered Hebes, surly Allegros and smirking Penserosos, usurp the place of truth, propriety and character.' There appeared a tract attacking the licentiousness of the Lely period under the title 'Just and Reasonable Reprehension of Naked Breasts and Shoulders.' Gaspar was to see and assist in this change. He had come over to England from Antwerp during the Civil War and

58. THOMAS PELHAM-HOLLES, 1ST DUKE OF NEWCASTLE, AND HENRY CLINTON, 7TH EARL OF LINCOLN

National Portrait Gallery (Kit Kat Collection)

had been introduced to General Lambert, himself an amateur artist of merit. At the time of the Restoration he had met Lely and was immediately engaged to work in his studio. Gaspar's task, once Lely had arranged his model and pose, was to draw in the picture. Then the master came back to make any alterations and start in detail on the drawing and painting of the face and hands and any other particular feature. Gaspar was handed from artist to artist, and when he died in 1691 he had painted postures for Kneller for some ten years. He himself was an adequate portrait painter, as is shown by the picture of Charles II with mathematical instruments at St. Bartholomew's Hospital and the *Hobbes* at Gresham College.

The painting of draperies was a long and slow business, and although Kneller, whether painting them himself or having them painted by the assistants at his command, favoured an impression of the design or material as opposed to the pin-point detail with the tip of the brush which had been customary in Tudor and Stuart painting, the ornate dresses and jewels nevertheless took a long time, and that is how the drapery painters came into the studio.

John James Backer was the nephew of Jacob A. Backer, a famous Dutch portrait painter of a previous generation and a brother of Adrian Backer, another painter, who lived between 1643 and 1686. John James's dates are uncertain, but it would appear that he was in England before Godfrey Kneller's arrival and worked in his studio till the end of the century; he accompanied Kneller when he went to Brussels to paint the Emperor of Bavaria in 1697. Walpole in his *Anecdotes* says that, unlike the other, Backer did not practise as a painter on his own, but this is incorrect, for there is an engraving by John Summer of a picture of Sir Stephen Fox by J. J. Backer.

Godfrey Kneller found a young Dutchman, John Pieters, a nephew of Pieter Eyckens the history painter; he was only eighteen when he arrived in England in 1685. Save for instructions from his father, the youth had little training, but he soon found himself employed as one of the leading drapery and background painters in Kneller's studio. He was a general handyman and did considerable work which included preparing and repairing canvases. According to Vertue, Pieters was with Kneller until 1712. Pieters, like Backer, had helped and assisted Vertue, who acknowledged this fact in his Notebooks. After leaving the studio Pieters took to drink, and though he obtained a little work repairing and patching up pictures he died poor and gouty in 1727.

The most versatile and varied of the assistants was the Frenchman, Marcel Laroon, who was born at The Hague in 1653 and appears to have gone straight to the north of England, where he practised in Yorkshire as a portrait painter. So successful was he that he decided to come down to London; there he found that there was not room for a somewhat second-rate portrait painter, but on account of his versatility he rapidly found work in Kneller's studio, and painted draperies for Godfrey until his death in 1702. It is not possible to differentiate between the draperies of Godfrey himself and his three first assistants, Backer,

Pieters and Laroon, but Laroon appears to have had a great facility for copying and imitating besides being able to draw well, so I should be inclined to treat him as the leading assistant. Besides assisting Kneller he painted history, portraits and conversation pieces. His power of imitating was at the time very good, and Walpole writes of his father having 'a picture by him that easily passed for Bassan's.' In addition he was a draughtsman and engraver, and published a book on fencing, the series known as Tempest's *Cries of London*, and a print of the coronation of William and Mary.

Jean Baptiste Monnoyer (59) and Henry Vergazon were painters working on their own who were called in from time to time to assist Kneller. Monnoyer's flowers—consisting usually of a vase on a pedestal with well-drawn flowers, one or two of which have dropped out and lie on the pedestal or at the foot—are unmistakable. His only rival in flower painting was Huysman, and Monnoyer appears to have eclipsed his Dutch competitor. Born at Lille in 1635, he studied in Paris and Antwerp, and before coming to England in Charles II's reign he worked in the Court of Louis XIV, and there are paintings of flowers by him, murals and otherwise, at Versailles and Vincennes. He was brought to London by the Duke of Montagu, after a visit to Paris by the latter, to decorate the second Montagu House, afterwards the British Museum, in about 1670, and worked in London until his death. His works can be found in nearly every collection dating back to this period in England, and he appears to have been most prolific. As already stated, the fashion for landscapes had not yet arrived, but Monnoyer introduced the vogue for still life. There are specimens of his work at Hampton Court and at Windsor. At the time of his death he was preparing a folio of eighty engravings of flowers, which was posthumously completed. Godfrey Kneller painted his head, which was engraved by White.

Whilst we know much about Monnoyer we know little about Henry Vergazon except that he was a Dutch landscape painter who specialized in ruins and castles and he died in France. Most of the dark buildings and ruins that appear in the earlier of Kneller's pictures, whether they were of Windsor, Knole, Athlone or some Roman fantasia, were by Vergazon. His colouring was very sombre, and though it is known that he painted some early landscapes I know of no single painting by him.

A general hack and assistant in the studio was Jacob Van der Roer (1648-1699), who came to England during Charles II's reign and entered Godfrey's studio about 1680. He was a portrait painter, but it appears that in the studio he lent a hand at everything, from painting in postures and basic mediums to detailed draperies and landscapes. He left about 1690 and died at Dort.

Though we have been reviewing various aspects of Godfrey's life, background, assistants and contemporaries, we have said little about his brother John Zachary, who had set up on his own in London; no doubt his relationship gave him *entrée* to many houses and families as a painter of frescoes, architectures and still life. He worked in his brother's studio, but his chief relationship with his brother was as a contemporary copyist, in miniature and in water-colour. A copyist to full scale was Fancatti, an Italian to whom may be attributed many of the bad contemporary versions which pass as Knellers.

So much for the earlier assistants. In about 1710 a young man entered the studio as a pupil and assistant. He was called James Worsdale, and legend has it that he was an illegitimate son of Godfrey; of this I have found no proof, but he was certainly an amusing character. He worked in the studio for some eight years or so until Godfrey found that he was secretly married to Lady Kneller's niece. When the fact was discovered he was flung out and sent to Ireland. Whilst in the studio Worsdale was a general assistant, and at the same time worked on his own, painting portraits or making copies of his master's work on private commission. We know from Pope that he had a picture of Atterbury by Kneller which he used to make Worsdale copy for three or four guineas. A contemporary record says 'whenever he wished to pay a compliment to one of his friends he gave him an "Original" picture of Atterbury.' Of the 'Originals' Worsdale had painted four or five.

After being turned out of the studio, Worsdale made a name for himself in Ireland. He was a convivial, amusing and sociable person, and though his pencil and brush alone might have led him nowhere, he became acquainted in Dublin with Lord Blarney and Lawrence Parsons, the first Earl of Rosse. Together with Lord Rosse he was founder of the Irish Hell Fire Club which met up in the Wicklow Hills, and for one of their members, Lord Santry, he painted a group of five. This picture, formerly at Santry Court, now hangs in the Dublin National Gallery. He also painted most of the nobility and Anglo-Irish of the period. His chief popularity arose some ten years after his master's death, between 1720 and 1745. When he could not obtain payment for a commissioned picture he used to chalk over the picture with intersected lines which made the subject appear behind bars. This he would exhibit as prominently as possible until the subject, through pride or shame, was compelled to pay for and purchase the work. Worsdale wrote a few ballads and plays.

There was a satire published in Dublin which read as follows:

> 'Tho' Worsdale is for satire too obscure,
> Must he uncensured artfully procure?
> Frequent, as Painter, to his employer's house,
> And thence deludes his mistress or his spouse?
> True to the lover's procreating cause
> He breaks all ties, all hospitable laws,
> And pimps, resistless, while his pencil draws.'

Worsdale instituted libel proceedings against the author, but lost his case, so it may well be assumed that the rhyme was a fair character sketch.

During the latter period he spent most of his time writing, and appeared himself in a ballad farce he wrote called *A Cure for a Scold*. Later he returned to England, where he became an actor, but Sir Robert Walpole managed to obtain him a situation as Master Painter to the Board of Ordnance, a sinecure, which Worsdale's son inherited on his death at the age of seventy-five in 1767.

He was buried at St. Paul's, Covent Garden, where his self-composed epitaph reads:

'Eager to get but not to keep the pelf,
A friend to all mankind except himself.'

There is a portrait of him by Pine which was engraved in mezzotint by William Dickinson; indeed, most of Worsdale's works are now only remembered by the engravings.

Edward and Robert Byng were the two assistants of the latter period. It was Edward Byng who informed Vertue of all the facts he recorded about Godfrey Kneller, and on his word has been based all the research in the subject from Vertue, Walpole, Ackerman and Collins Baker, besides other historians and writers enquiring into the period.

What Byng did leave us, as the result of Godfrey's will, was a very large number of pictures which he had completed for Kneller and may well have worked on almost from the start. Byng is responsible for the many later Knellers which with the bad contemporary copies have detracted from his real reputation.

Kneller often included animals in his pictures, whether a small deer, as in the Sackville children's picture at Knole (46) or the white horse on which William III rides in triumph (25). I think he usually painted these himself, but J. J. Backer may have painted the earlier horses, for, as we know, he went to Brussels with Godfrey in 1697 and the picture Kneller painted was of the Emperor on a white horse. Kneller certainly liked painting animals, as appears from some of his drawings as well as from the picture of the *Greyhound* in possession of Sir Godfrey Thomas at St. James's Palace (50), Lord Buckhurst's deer, or the lizard at the foot of Miss Pitt in the *Hampton Court Beauties*.

To work as Godfrey did, assistants were essential. The artist of to-day, especially the portrait painter, may well abhor those methods, but the number of hands and eyes which went to make one entity was necessary in order to meet the requirements of the time. Kneller owes much to his assistants. Though their names are forgotten with the exception of Monnoyer, without them he would never have left his mark. Where he was often at fault was in accepting bad work from them, for several pictures I have seen consist of a good head and pose spoilt by bad drapery and background.

59. JEAN BAPTISTE MONNOYER

Engraved by G. White

60. JOHN SMITH

Engraved by J. Smith (1716)

61. MISS VOSS AS ST. AGNES

Engraved by J. Smith (1716)

CHAPTER VIII

KNELLER AND THE EARLY MEZZOTINT ARTISTS

If it had not been for the English and Irish mezzotinters many of Godfrey Kneller's works would now be untraceable. The presence of this extremely fine method of contemporary reproduction makes possible a rapid study of the art of Godfrey Kneller, though without the benefit of colour. Further, the mezzotints which are so often dated—at any rate as far as publication is concerned—are of immense value in dating pictures where they were unsigned, or where there is no other method of fixing the approximate period during his long life in which the original work was produced.

Mezzotint until recent years had been the most efficient and artistic method of reproducing works of art, as may be seen from the plates in this book. Where a mezzotint is produced instead of the original painting, little of the drawing and composition is lost. To make it quite clear, I should perhaps explain the difference, first between an engraving and an etching, and then between those two and mezzotint. The method of reproducing both engraving and etching, whether they be on copper or steel plate, is that after the design has been drawn, the plates are dipped in acid so that the picture is further strengthened and clarified by the acid eating into wherever the plate has been penetrated by the etcher's or engraver's tool. An engraver works by cutting into the plate in a straightforward manner and the picture is made up of a series of lines; whilst the etcher works on the point and his effect is produced by a collection of dots. In both these methods, owing to the plates being dipped in acid and the drawing being firm and metallic, many impressions can be taken, but there is a hardness in the final result.

In both normal line engraving and etching the artist works from a smooth surface and reproduces his shade from a plate which would print uniformly white if it was not scratched. Herein lies the difference with the mezzotint artist, who works from a rough surface and thus reproduces his lights and shades from a plate which is uniformly dark. Further, the plate is not dipped or cleaned in acid. In earliest times all mezzotint plates were of copper and these are still the best, though modern methods have enabled mezzotints of a harder and coarser nature resembling line engravings to be produced from steel plates.

The plate is first prepared by using what is known as a cradle. This cradle, which marks the plate with little points or dashes, is worked in a mathematical manner across the plate; this is done by dividing the plate into squares. The artist then works the cradle first from left to right, then from top to bottom, then diagonally from top left to bottom right, until the square has been worked in as many as thirty-six different directions. Instead of the normal hand-scraper, a

K

circular file with points instead of grooves may be worked over the plate. If a plate was completely worked over with the scraper and completely prepared and an impression was taken before the artist had commenced to put on the picture, the effect would be to produce a black velvet-like print. Having prepared the plate, the artist then engraves the impression, using a scraper for the deeper colours and a burnisher for the higher lights. As he cuts into this plate not only does he push down into it but at the same time the scraper pushes up the side, thus giving the high lights. This burr—as the little rim or area which is pushed up is called— gives the soft and tender appearance which is so noticeable in mezzotint, for instance on the high lights on the faces. It is, however, delicate, and the number of impressions that can be taken from a mezzotint plate is limited—unlike the engraver's plate, which is burnt in by acid.

On the Continent mezzotint is usually known as the 'English method' of engraving. This is due to a belief held well into the last century that it was a method originated by John Evelyn the diarist or by Prince Rupert. This is not correct, and the researches of such men as Laborde have confirmed that the originator of the method was a Dutchman, but it was in England that the manner was first developed on a large scale, although disciples of the new method did go off into Europe.

The inventor of the method was Ludwig von Siegen, a soldier, who was an amateur engraver when off duty. He was born in 1609 and educated in Holland, became Kammerjunker to the Landgrave of Hesse-Cassel and in the year 1642 was residing at Amsterdam. In that year he completed a portrait of Amelia the Dowager Landgravine in a new method of engraving after a drawing which he had done from life shortly before. Von Siegen dedicated the plate to his master the Landgrave, and Léon de Laborde in 1839 found the dedicatory letter, of which I will reproduce extracts, as it confirms the earliest known details of mezzotint engraving.

Von Siegen wrote:

'This is a print from copper, Gracious Prince and Lord, which I promised to prepare for the ever praiseworthy memory of your Grace's mother, in order that many illustrious persons acquainted with the actions of so widely famed a princess, might be enabled to possess the likeness of her person.

But since I have discovered a new or singular invention of a kind never before beheld, I have, on account of the nicety of the work, been able only to have a few copies struck off, not thousands, as in the case of ordinary engravings and therefore can with them only oblige a few persons. . . .

How this work has been done on copper plate no engraver or artist can explain or imagine for, as your Grace is aware, only three methods of engraving on copper have hitherto been seen: (1) Engraving or touching in line, (2) Etching or touching with the point, (3) A method hitherto very uncommon called puncturing, also executed entirely with points, but in a different manner, and with great labour, and therefore unusual. The present method is however none of these, although here also are merely little points and not a single line or stroke; though in some places it appears like a line, yet it is all merely dots, which information I did not wish to conceal from your Grace as well skilled in art.'

This letter was dated 19/20 August 1642. The next year Siegen published a portrait after Honthorst, and the following year a portrait of Prince William of Orange and his Consort.

In about 1654, when the English Court was in exile, Prince Rupert, James I's grandson by his daughter Elizabeth and Frederick Prince Palatine, met Siegen in Brussels. They were both soldiers and artists, and Siegen must have passed his secret on to Prince Rupert, who in the year 1656 produced his now famous and historical plate called *The Great Executioner*. During the four years prior to the Restoration and the return of the Court to England, Prince Rupert practised the art of engraving in Brussels and communicated the secret to one Wallerant Vaillant (1623-77), who later practised as a mezzotint artist in Amsterdam.

The 'secret' of mezzotint or dry point is perhaps a misnomer, for although historians like to make a mystery of it, I believe that Siegen, being only an amateur, communicated the method to anyone who might be interested and Prince Rupert did not, as some suggest, break a confidence by passing on the method. John Evelyn wrote in the *Sculptura* in 1662:

'His Highness (Prince Rupert) did indulge me the liberty of publishing the whole manner and dress of his new way of engraving with a freedom perfectly generous and obliging. But when I had well considered it (so much having already been expressed, which may suffice to give the hint to all ingenious persons how it is to be performed) I did not think it necessary that an art so curious, and (as yet) so little vulgar (and which indeed does not succeed where the workman is not an accomplished designer and has a competent talent in painting likewise) was to be prostituted at so cheap a rate, as the more naked describing of it here, would too soon have exposed it to.'

Evelyn was frequently pompous and rather foolish, and I would believe that he alone was making a mystery of the matter. However, this reference in 1662 for a long while caused people to think Prince Rupert invented the method, but it only proves that he had brought it to England by that year.

In the year 1669 a nineteen-year-old boy (he may have been older), William Sherwin, published the earliest known mezzotint in England—a portrait of Charles II, a half-length in an oval frame with large wig, white cravat and collar of the Garter badge on his left shoulder. Sherwin died in 1714 and produced many plates between his first one and his death, although only one can be traced after a portrait of Godfrey Kneller—a half-length of Henry, Duke of Beaufort.

A glance at Appendix D 1 will show the importance of the mezzotint engravers to Kneller. There are at least 400 plates engraved in dry point after Kneller by over 40 different artists. A very large number were done during Godfrey's lifetime and some very soon afterwards, as is the case with John Faber Junior's Kit Kat series published in 1735. Appendix D 2 shows at a glance the principal mezzotint engravers during Godfrey Kneller's lifetime.

The first engraver to devote himself to reproducing the works of Godfrey Kneller on any large scale was Isaac Beckett, who was born in Kent in 1653. He was apprenticed to a calico printer but when in London met Luttrell, the Dublin-born engraver, who arrived in England about 1670 when only twenty, with the intention of studying law. Luttrell had a gift for drawing which he practised as a portrait artist in crayon; he was the forerunner of the Irish school of mezzotint artists which flourished in the first half of the eighteenth century under Andrew Miller, Thomas Beard, John Brooks and McArdell, but their work is outside the scope of this book. Luttrell had turned to mezzotint work in about 1680, and Isaac Beckett, having seen an early plate by him, forsook calico printing for the dry-pointer's copper. Luttrell himself worked until 1710, when he died. Isaac Beckett seems only to have worked between 1681 and 1688, but within that period he produced over 100 plates, besides printing and publishing the plates of other workers up till the time of his death in about 1715.

To Beckett we owe the publication of 28 plates after the early English works of Godfrey Kneller, which include the half-length of Sir Godfrey himself taken from a self-portrait showing him as a man between thirty-five and forty. This plate is that shown in the early editions of Walpole's work and is after a portrait formerly in Walpole's collection and now in the possession of Lord Derby at Knowsley. To Beckett we owe the popular plates of the last Stuart days; apart from Charles II and James II his 28 plates after Kneller include the favourites Cleveland and Portsmouth and the attractive *Lord Wriothesley Russell* (45), also *Potemkin* (63).

Beckett's plates are noticeable for the care with which he prepared the ground and his fine and high finishes. Despite the monochrome he manages to obtain the most realistic effect with his lights.

His disappearance as an engraver after 1688 may well be on account of his marriage to a lady of fortune, but he will be remembered as the first Englishman who practised engraving extensively.

When Godfrey arrived in England, besides William Sherwin only Abraham Blooteling was working in mezzotint. Blooteling, who had been born in Amsterdam in 1634, came over to England in 1674. He is reputed to have left again in 1676, but in view of the fact that he engraved *Peter John Potemkin*, the Russian Ambassador, after Kneller, he cannot have left until after 1683 when the picture was painted. Blooteling may well have engraved some of his works after his return to Amsterdam from sketches made in England, but before doing so he must have seen the original paintings during his visit. Blooteling also worked in 'line,' but of his 128 recorded mezzotints only some 20 were worked and published in England. *Potemkin* was his only reproduction after Kneller, and I think must have been Kneller's first work so recorded.

After 1680 until the turn of the century, other than Beckett the chief workers in mezzotint were R. White, R. Williams, Bernard Lens Junior, William Faithorne and John Smith. White, Williams and Faithorne each worked about six plates after Kneller, whilst John Smith was the chief successor to Beckett. Between 1690 and his death in 1720 Smith engraved and published 140 of Kneller's pictures, whereas Bernard Lens (1659-1725), who engraved between 1680 and

62. THOMAS BETTERTON

Engraved by R. Williams

63. PETER JOHN POTEMKIN, RUSSIAN AMBASSADOR

Engraved by Isaac Beckett (1682)

65. JAMES CRAGGS

Engraved by J. Simon (1720)

64. SIR JOHN VANBRUGH

Engraved by J. Faber, Junior

1710, only did one work after Kneller, but is of interest in that he was the son of the enameller of the same name who was a friend of Godfrey's and father of the miniature painter—also a Bernard Lens.

Robert White was an engraver and worked in portraiture in pencil on vellum. He was London-born and lived from 1645 to 1704. Owing to his having the same initials as Williams, their plates are confused and the manner of working is similar; and they were both engraving at the same period. His plates after Kneller include the excellent *Isabella, Duchess of Grafton*.

Of R. Williams we know little—not even his Christian name—but it appears as his name denotes that he was a Welshman who practised engraving in London between 1680 and 1704. Like White, his works are reminiscent of Beckett and they are all bold and masterly. His six plates after Kneller include a half-length in an oval of Thomas Betterton, the tragedian (1635-1710), which is much sought after by collectors (62). Williams appears to have concentrated on the works of William Wissing rather than on those of Kneller.

William Faithorne, who worked between 1680 and 1710, was particularly successful with women, although except for *Mary II* his Kneller portraits were of men and included three plates of *William III* (66) besides one of *James, Duke of Ormonde*.

John Smith (60), who began engraving in 1690, was the most prolific engraver of Kneller's works. His 140 plates numbered 40 more than those of John Faber, who, as we shall see, recorded the Kit Kat series, besides the *Hampton Court Beauties*.

A pupil of Beckett, Smith is remarkable for the brilliancy of his effects. His plates are clear and powerful, besides being meticulously correct in drawing, and therefore of great value to the student. Challoner Smith thinks Smith more metallic than Simon the Frenchman, but this to my mind is not so—Smith appears to have a clearness yet tenderness in his work which has not been equalled.

To Smith we are grateful for four plates of family interest to Godfrey, though strangely enough he did no plate of the painter himself. The plates are those of Mrs. Voss and her child, that is of Kneller's mistress and daughter (28), and three other plates of Kneller's daughter, one as Miss Voss and two as St. Agnes (61).

Smith's works include nearly all Kneller's most eminent portraits, and amongst the best plates is that at Knole of *Lionel, Lord Buckhurst* and *Lady Mary Sackville, Grinling Gibbons* (71) and *Vanbrugh* (64). In addition to his own originals, Smith retouched and published plates after Beckett, Lens, Simon and Williams.

The French influence was brought into mezzotint by John Simon, who was born in Charenton in 1675 and came to England as a Protestant refugee in 1708, when he began engraving. He was John Smith's chief rival and in the last year superseded him as far as Kneller was concerned. Simon's work is individual; his grounding was less close than Smith's, with the result that the finished prints are less brilliant. There are over 40 plates by Simon after Kneller, nearly all of the later period; they include *George I as King*, *George II as Prince of Wales* and *James Craggs* (65).

L

At about the same time as John Simon came from France, John Faber, who had come from Holland in 1695, as a miniaturist, opened his publishing and print shop at the Savoy. Faber Senior specialised in prints of Dissenting clergy, but there are six plates of his after Kneller and they include the three-quarter length of *Admiral George Byng* of the Greenwich series, and the best *John Dryden* (4) which was one of a set of four men of letters which included *Chaucer, Ben Jonson* and *Samuel Butler*. But it is John Faber Junior to whom, after John Smith, we are most indebted. Born about 1684, he came to England with his father when a small boy, and worked from 1712 until his death in 1756. His most prolific period was after Kneller's death, between 1730 and 1740. Although he learned his trade from his father, he worked quite independently of him; after a training in his father's studio, he worked for a while with John Smith and also under Vanderbank in the Academy. His early portraits before Godfrey's death are scarce and rare, but in the later period his work was bold and finished. It is of interest to note that he was a Freemason, which resulted in his specializing in their portraits rather as his father had done in Dissenting clergy. His plates include two of *Godfrey Kneller*, one introduces his set of twelve *Hampton Court Beauties* (13); the frontispiece of this series shows Kneller in an oval frame turned towards the left, and looking to the front. It is of the same period as the portrait frontispiece to the Kit Kat series, which is after the small painting which hangs with the Kit Kat portraits and similar to that in the Uffizi.

In addition to the *Beauties* and the fine Kit Kat series, John Faber published the *Chinese Convert* from Kensington and a head and shoulder of *Alexander Pope* in profile looking right (72). Faber's best known print is that of *Pope*, after Van Loo, a three-quarter length seated of Pope as an old man.

Robert White's son George began work at about the same time as Faber Junior. White used a method of etching-in his subjects before grounding; he also tried to increase the intensity of lights with the graver, but this was not effective when plates became slightly worn. There is a clear plate of *Jean Baptiste Monnoyer*, the flower painter, after Kneller which is reproduced by Walpole, who says it is after a portrait at Houghton which he owned (59). A search at Houghton failed to reveal the original painting and I cannot trace it from the Strawberry Hill Sale, and so it must have gone to St. Petersburg with the Houghton pictures. White's *Pope*, reputed to have been painted in 1723, would therefore be one of Kneller's last portraits. It is a half-length sitting directed towards the front and looking downwards. Pope wears a cap, open collar and loose gown; his left elbow leans on a book and his right hand supports his forehead.

To go further into the mezzotinters after Kneller would only be of interest to the expert, who is advised to study the meticulously full details of Challoner Smith, but mention should be made of Andrew Miller, a pupil of Faber's, whose prints are now rare. But, as stated earlier in this chapter, he returned to Ireland, and is known to have been established in what is now St. Andrew Street, Dublin, known in 1744 as Hog's Hill. Miller's plates after Kneller were mostly copied

66. WILLIAM III   *Engraved by W. Faithorne*

67. MARY II   *Engraved by J. Beckett*

69. GEORGE I

Engraved by John Simon (1717)

68. GEORGE II AS PRINCE OF WALES

Engraved by John Smith (1714)

from other engravers, but he introduced a new and virile style into mezzotinting, which had declined after 1740. A word too should be said about Peter Pelham (1680-1751), who began engraving in 1720 but left England and settled with his wife and family in Boston in 1726, thus preceding Smibert the painter and preparing the way for both portraiture and engraving in America. Besides engraving he also painted, and there is a record of a portrait by him of the Rev. John Mather painted in America in 1727. In addition to introducing contemporary portraiture he engraved and published plates after the Italian classical painters, thus also bringing that art of continental Europe to America. He had a son J. C. Pelham, born in 1721, who painted in America, and his wife by second marriage, Mrs. Mary Copley, was the mother of John Singleton Copley, R.A.

This hurried survey of the methods of mezzotinters, their development and the work of Kneller's contemporaries, will, I hope, prove their value, but it is only by studying them individually that their real merit can be ascertained. As I write the mezzotint is out of fashion with the collector, as is shown by the sale-room prices, but when they are good they have all the feeling and charm of any original. Later, with the development of aquatint, they might be coloured, but in the period which interests us they were in monochrome.

Without the mezzotints Kneller's name might well have been forgotten except by the owner of family portraits. It is hard to pick up an historical book or biography of the period without finding illustrations in mezzotint after Kneller by Beckett, Smith, Faber Junior, the Whites and others that I have mentioned. Others I have omitted for lack of space, though they are included in Appendix D 1, play a very full and important part in the diffusion of his art.

Whilst the works of Kneller may be expensive to collect and too large for many a modern house, the mezzotints give great scope to the small collector. The student may study them in the collections at the British Museum, Victoria and Albert Museum, the Pepysian Collection at Magdalene College, Cambridge, and the Fitzwilliam Museum, in the Storer Collection at Eton College and the Joly Collection at the Royal Dublin Society.

Although a number of Kneller's works were engraved by men such as George Vertue, whose Notebooks have been quoted, it was in mezzotint that he was chiefly reproduced, and I therefore intend to spend no time on the other engravers, who were of little importance.

CHAPTER IX

KNELLER AND THE POETS

THE fact that Godfrey Kneller knew most of the leading literary men of his period is borne out by the many portraits of them that he painted; but then this may well be said of any successful painter of any period. Godfrey, with his gift of repartee and wit, found himself very much the centre of the literary world. He acted as a neutral or pivot in a country divided against itself on the question of royal succession to the throne from the time of his arrival in England until his death; it was the period when the great Whig and Tory parties were taking shape and at a time over one hundred years after the Reformation, when religious intolerance once more predominated as the persecuted Catholics tried to raise their heads to regain their right of equality—a right they did not regain until the nineteenth century.

The relationship of a painter to his subject is usually that of the hirer and hired, but in the case of most of Godfrey's more eminent subjects it was a relationship of friend to friend. To-day certain foreign artists—especially those of the theatre —find it easy to enter the most select London society. The same was true of Godfrey, who with his push, boastfulness, self-confidence and snob tendencies found his way into the highest and most select company.

The poets of Godfrey's period were in a unique position for they held a status of trust and eminence. They were not regarded as strange freaks. They were the champions of their cause, using the poet's rhyme rather than the newspaper or the radio to spread their propaganda through the country. Further, they were nearly all of what in Victorian days would have been called the upper or middle classes. To be a poet it was necessary to have small means of one's own besides a good education, especially in the classics. At the end of the seventeenth century a good education was only available to those who could afford to pay for it. The poet therefore, whether the son of a nobleman or a merchant, began his career with the advantage of education and a definite position in contemporary society. During Godfrey's life in England, with the growth of the political feeling there increased also the party propaganda which resulted in the earliest journals such as the *Spectator*, *Tatler*, or the Whig or Tory *Examiner*. So it was that most of the poets after 1700 were also journalists or pamphleteers. The development of the journal, though at first they were only weeklies or thrice-weeklies, makes it far easier for the student of the period to follow the social and political life of the time as told by eye-witnesses. Added to the journals there were also the great diarists, Evelyn and Pepys, besides memoir-writers such as Grammont. It is an age in which the study of the background is simple, but that of the individual is difficult owing to the political prejudices resulting in inaccuracies and mis-statements.

In an earlier chapter I traced briefly the political background of the period, and I would recall that Kneller came to England only sixteen years after the Restoration, when High Churchmen were in power, and saw James II—the last Roman Catholic monarch—arrive and depart. This was followed by the Succession trouble, which eventually brought the Hanoverians to the throne and the Whigs to power for the greater part of the eighteenth century. In his time personal animosity, still not forgotten by the contemporaries of his and his father's generation during civil war, and daily kindled by plot and intrigues, was very pronounced. It is for this reason that we are interested to find after 1700 that the great Whigs such as Addison, Steele, Tickell and Congreve were to be met at Godfrey's house at Great Queen Street or at Twickenham along with the great Tories, Swift, Prior, Arbuthnot, Gay and Pope.

The first literary figure with whom Godfrey Kneller came in contact was John Dryden (1631-1700). Besides painting his portrait on several occasions—there are versions in the National Portrait Gallery and at Trinity College, Cambridge—Godfrey painted for Dryden a head of Shakespeare after one belonging to Lord Halifax, for which Dryden repaid him in the following verse:

> 'Shadows are but privations of the light,
> Yet when we walk, they shoot before the sight,
> With us approach, retire, arise and fall;
> Nothing themselves, and yet expressing all.
> Such are thy pieces imitating life,
> So near they almost conquer in the strife,
> And from their animated canvas came,
> Demanding souls, loosened from the frame.'

Dryden, as Restoration playwright, was the official writer of plays for the King when Godfrey arrived in England. There is little doubt that they met during the first few years of Godfrey's stay. At this time John Dryden was trying to imitate and improve on the Elizabethans, and in 1674 he had published his *Troilus and Cressida*.

He wrote of himself:

'. . . My conversation is slow and dull, my humour saturnine and reserved; in short, I am none of those who endeavour to break jests in company or make repartees.'

After the accession of William and Mary, Dryden, who had become a Roman Catholic in 1685, had been dismissed from his Court position. He found himself the central figure among those who met at Will's Coffee House, where the company included Vanbrugh the architect and playwright, and the future Whig writers Congreve and Addison. Legend has it that Pope, at the age of about ten, was taken to see the great Dryden at Will's, but precocious as Pope was this is not very likely, though he may well have seen him walking to or from this house in the same way as one has heard Liberals recall childhood glimpses of Gladstone and Tories of Disraeli. It was during this period that Dryden produced the *Hind and the Panther*, an ingenious argument for Roman Catholicism put into the mouth of a ' milk white hind, immortal and unchanged.' This was to be refuted a few years later by the story of the *Country Mouse and Town Mouse* by Kneller's friends Matthew Prior and Montagu, the future Lord Halifax.

John Evelyn (1620-1706) and Samuel Pepys (1633-1703), the famous diarists, became good friends of Godfrey Kneller during his early years in England.

Evelyn's diaries, which cover the period 1640-1706, contain three references to Godfrey Kneller:

'1685 October 8. I had my picture drawn this week by the famous Kneller.

1689 June 9. Visited Dr. Burnett, now Bishop of Sarum; got him to let Mr. Kneller draw his picture.

July 8th. I sat for my picture to Mr. Kneller, for Mr. Pepys, late Secretary to the Admiralty, holding my *Sylva* in my right hand. It was at his long and earnest request and is placed in his library. Kneller never painted in a more masterly manner.'

These entries are of vital interest. The 1685 reference already claims Godfrey as 'famous.' The first reference in 1689 dates the *Dr. Burnett* at the Charterhouse, whilst the latter refers to the famous and perhaps one of the best of the pictures which now hang in the Royal Society's Rooms at Burlington House. Evelyn's *Sylva* was a plea for reafforestation inspired by the prevalent destruction and cutting of forests for glass-blowing and other new industries. Unlike Pepys, John Evelyn concurred with the changes of religion and politics and therefore remained in favour until his death. It is interesting to note that he let his house with its beautiful garden at Deptford to Admiral John Benbow, whose portrait by Kneller hangs at Greenwich. Benbow sublet it to Peter the Great when he visited England to inspect the Deptford Dockyard in 1698, and Godfrey went down there to paint the fine picture of this monarch which now hangs at Kensington Palace (75).

Samuel Pepys's *Diary* contains no reference to Kneller, for, unlike Evelyn's, his only covers the short period before Godfrey's arrival—in the years immediately following the Restoration, 1660-64.

We learn of Pepys's relationship with Kneller through his correspondence. John Evelyn described Pepys as 'a worthy, industrious and curious person,' and his *Diary*, as all who have read will agree, is far more entertaining and intimate than Evelyn's. Pepys made his name as Secretary to the Navy and published his *Memoirs of the Navy* in 1690. He would still be remembered in this naval connection had his *Diary* never been published. Evelyn, but for the diaries which were published in 1818, would now be forgotten.

Both Evelyn and Kneller were early Fellows of the Royal Society, and the picture referred to on 8th July 1689 found its way next year into that Society's collection when Pepys became its President. The Society also owns the very fine

70. JOHN LOCKE (1704)

71. GRINLING GIBBONS

Engraved by J. Smith

head of Pepys by Kneller. There is another fine one by him in the Hall at Magdalene College, Cambridge, where Pepys's Library is now lodged. Another picture of a younger Pepys by Lely hangs in the Library, and Greenwich has yet another of him by Kneller.

Although Pepys was a Cambridge man, it was ever his desire to pay a compliment to the University of Oxford, hence we have the major Pepys-Kneller correspondence.

In about 1701 Pepys decided that he would present the University of Oxford with a picture of the eighty-five-year-old mathematician, John Wallis, and owing to Wallis's age Kneller went down to Oxford to do this work. John Wallis had written to Pepys that, had he not been so old, he would willingly have gone to London, but in the circumstances he would show his great appreciation of the honour being accorded him by treating Kneller with 'the respect due to a person of his quality.'

On completion of the picture in March 1702, which was finished off in London, Kneller wrote to tell Pepys that—

'I never did a better picture, nor so good a one in my life, which is the opinion of all that have seen it.'

On hearing that it was completed, Pepys appeared a little piqued that he had not been kept informed of its progress. To this Kneller replied very pompously that definite instructions had been conveyed to him by Dr. Charlett, the Vice-Chancellor, or else 'I should hardly have left my home and business for Oxford conversation's sake'; the trifling trouble was settled when Pepys assured Kneller that he was satisfied with the picture, and later in the year Kneller wrote the following letter to Pepys:

'SIR,—I understand you have a frame amaking for that picture which I desire to see put on at my house and all packed together in a case safe, for I intend to send my servant with it to Oxford, for to place it and look that no damage may appear.

And I will when you please send the porters for to fetch it, and varnish it well before it goes, and finish all to the utmost of my skill.

I believe Mrs. Skinner's picture is in the house, locked up with others by my brother as he is gone away for a month or six weeks to the Bath, before you desired that picture. Pray, give my humble respects to Madame Skinner and command, Sir,

Yours faithfully humble servant,

G. KNELLER.'

In August Dr. Charlett heard that the picture was due shortly to arrive at Oxford and wrote to Pepys:

'I am glad that it is so admirably done, though I doubt not, besides the point of good manners, your judgment might have added to the beauty of the contrivance but the Painter's fancy was warm, and his imagination not to be controlled it seems with delays.'

Samuel Pepys replied:

'REVEREND SIR,—Sir Godfrey Kneller has (according to what I told you last night) put his best hand to our picture, and seems equally satisfied concerning it with respect both to the piece itself and to the dresse I have put into it, and so I hope you and all your learned friends about will be pleased and at least I have done my best towards it. Nor let its coming in a lacquered frame lead you to think otherwise, for I could have sent it in the same with my Lord of Ormonde's gilt for less money. But I was led to it by the advice of Sir G. Kneller's own man, in consideration of its first lustre being nothing inferior to that of gold, and it being for ever kept so (when time shall tarnish it) at the 20th part of the charge and trouble that gold will. An observation confirmed by 40 years experience of my own. Nevertheless, if you or any of the gentlemen with you be of another minde, I shall most willingly before it be set up or at anytime hereafter during my life, whenever the University shall be pleased to desire it; which pray make knowne to it as you shall see proper.'

This correspondence is interesting not only for recording how the picture of Wallis which now hangs in the Bodleian was acquired but as giving an insight into Kneller's methods. It seems obvious that he was a little nervous of Pepys's criticism; content with flattery, Kneller did not like painting if the criticism was adverse. At the same time it shows Pepys very much the diplomat in handling the situation, but at the same time perhaps a little vexed, fancying himself as an amateur and patron of art, for not being consulted as the picture progressed.

It is interesting to note that among the Bodleian notes of the year 1701-2 is a receipt 'Paid to Sir Godfrey Kneller's man for varnishing two pictures of the Duke of Ormonde £2. 3. 0.' This man may well have been one of the assistants about whom we have written, but the note does show that, unlike the portrait painter of to-day, Kneller did not set out unassisted, for this varnishing was done at the same time as the *Wallis* picture.

Later, as the result of his work at Oxford, Kneller received an Honorary Degree of D.C.L.

Another friend whom Kneller made before 1700 was the playwright and actor Joseph Harris, who died in 1702 at the age of forty. In 1690 he had dedicated to Kneller his *Tragic Comedy Mistakes or False Reports* in which Dryden, besides Nahum Tate (1652-1715) and William Mountfort (1664-92), had assisted him.

In a little book published in the last century, by a conservative-minded gentleman who remained anonymous, I found an entry which read:

'Addison and Steele were attracted to that painting room (Kneller's in Great Queen Street) by their idleness and love of character, and by their love of hearing, seeing and knowing all that was going on in the great world.'

This is a very fair résumé of the relationship, for there was no doubt that most of the news and gossip, whether it was of the world of art, society or the Court, passed through the fashionable painter's studio. All the celebrities of the day passed through it, and with them they brought their news, which they handed on to Godfrey as he painted and Steele and Addison watched and flattered.

Joseph Addison (1672-1719) and Richard Steele (1672-1729) were both born the same year and educated at Charterhouse. Steele spent his early youth in Dublin, which doubtless gave him the tinge of humour with which his papers and satires are sprinkled. Both became staunch Whigs and friends of Sir Godfrey.

Addison's friendship with Kneller dates from the beginning of the eighteenth century when he was writing prior to an official appointment in Ireland under Lord Wharton the Viceroy. Then in 1709 Steele began his *Spectator*, which was followed by the *Tatler*. Steele was impudent, impulsive, even ostentatious and generous, and was very similar in character to Godfrey, whilst Addison was of soberer mood. It was not until his later days that Addison once again resumed the writing of poetry, and though perhaps a trifling poem the new lines were at least full of fancy and imagination. They were written to Sir Godfrey on his picture of George I, and I give them in full so that they may be duly appreciated.

'Kneller, with silence and surprise
We see Britannia's Monarch rise,
A godlike form, by thee displayed,
In all the force of light and shade,
And, aw'd by thy delusive hand,
As in the presence-chamber stand.
The magic of thy art calls forth
His secret soul and hidden worth,
His probity and mildness shows
His care of friends and scorn of foes;
In every stroke, in every line,
Does some exalted virtue shine,
And Albion's happiness we trace
Through all the features of his face.
    O may I live to hail the day,
When the glad nation shall survey
Their Sov'reign, through his wide command
Passing in progress o'er the land;
Each heart shall bend, and every voice
In loud applauding shouts rejoice,
Whilst all his gracious aspect praise,
And crowds grow loyal as they gaze.
    This image on the medal placed,
With its bright round of titles graced,
And stampt on British coins shall live
To richest ores the value give,
Or, wrought within the curious mould,
Shape and adorn the running gold.
    To bear this form the genial sun
Has daily, since his course begun,
Rejoiced the metal to refine,
And ripened the Peruvian mine.
    Thou, Kneller, long with noble pride,
The foremost of thy art hast vied
With nature in a generous strife,
And touched the canvas into life.
Thy pencil has, by monarch sought,
From reign to reign in ermine wrought,
And in their robes of state array'd
The Kings of half an age display'd.

Here swarthy Charles appears, and there
His brother with dejected air;
Triumphant Nassau here we find,
And with him Maria join'd;
There Anna, great as when she sent
Her armies through the continent,
Ere yet her Hero was disgrac'd;
O may fam'd Brunswick be the last,
(Though Heaven should with my wish agree)
And long preserve thy art in thee,
The last, the happiest British King
Whom thou shall paint or I shall sing:
　Wise Phidias, thus his skill to prove,
Through many a God advanced to Jove,
And taught the polisht rocks to shine
With airs and lineaments divine;
'Till Greece, amaz'd and half afraid,
Th' assembled deities surveyed.
　Great Pan, who wont to chase the fair,
And lov'd the spreading oak, was there;
Old Saturn too with upcast eyes
Beheld his abdicated skies;
And mighty Mars, for war renowned,
In adamantine armour frown'd;
By his the childless goddess rose
Minerva, studious to compose
Her twisted threads; the webb she strung,
And o'er a loom of marble hung;
Thetis, the troubled ocean's Queen,
Matched with a mortal next was seen,
Reclining on a funeral urn,
Her short liv'd darling Son to mourn.
The last was he, whose thunder lews
The Titan race, a rebel crew,
That from a hundred hills ally'd
In impious leagues, their King defy'd.
　This wonder of the sculptor's hand
Produced, his art was at a stand:
For who would hope new fame to raise,
Or risque his well established praise
That his high genius to approve,
Had drawn a George or carved a Jove.'

Though dated and perhaps rather trivial, this poem gives a very clear historical survey of Kneller's time and is amusing with its reference to Charles II:

'Great Pan, who wont to chase the fair,
　And lov'd the spreading oak, was there';

and to James II:

'Old Saturn too with upcast eyes
　Beheld his abdicated skies';

whilst Mary is compared to Minerva the 'childless Goddess,' William to 'Mars,' and finally Anne to 'Thetis . . . matched with a mortal . . . her short liv'd darling Son to mourn.'

Addison had an assistant who later was his executor although only four years his junior. He was called Thomas Tickell (1686-1740) and he followed Addison and Steele into Kneller's entourage of Whigs. But whilst we should not expect Masefield to-day to write a poem in praise of Gerald Kelly's Royal Portraits, or Auden to write a poem to Augustus John at his country seat at Fordingbridge, Thomas Tickell did this for Kneller, and the poem which was printed by Jacob Tonson in 1722, just a year before Godfrey's death, shows very well the position which the great painter had attained. It is a poem full of eulogies, but I feel perhaps Thomas Tickell may have had his tongue just slightly in his cheek when writing.

'*To Sir Godfrey Kneller at his Country Seat:*

To Whitton's shades and Hounslow's airy plain,
Then Kneller, tak'st thy Summer flight in vain;
In vain thy wish gives all the rural hours
To the fair Villa and well ordered bowers
To court thy pencil, early at thy gates
Ambition knocks and fleeting beauty waits;
The boastful Muse, of others' fame so sure,
Implores thy aid to make her own secure;

The great, the fair and (if ought nobler be,
Ought more belov'd) the arts solicit thee.

How can'st thou hope to fly the world? in vain
From Europe sever'd by the circling Main,
Sought by the Kings of every distant land
And every hero, worthy of thy hand.
Hast thou forgot that might Bourbon fear'd
He still was mortal till thy draught appear'd,
That Cosmo chose thy glowing form to place
Amid his masters of th' Lombard race?
See on her Titian's and her Guido's urns
Her failing Arts forlorn Hesperia mournes,
While Britain wins each garland from her brow,
Her wit and freedom first, her painting now.
Let the faint copier on old Tyber's shore
(Nor mean the task) each breathing must explore,
Line after line with painful patience trace
This Roman grandeur, that Athenian Grace.
Vain care of parts: if impotent of soul,
Th' industrious workman fails to warm the whole,
Each theft betrays the mark from whence it came,
And a cold stature stiffens in the frame,
Thee nature taught nor art her aid deny'd
(The kindest mistress and the surest guide)

69

To catch a likeness at one piercing sight,
And place the fairest in the fairest light.
Ere yet thy pencil tries her nicer toils
Or on the palette lie the blended oils
Thy careless chalk has left achieved thy Art
And her just image makes Cleora start.

A mind that grasps the whole, is rarely found,
Half learn'd, half painter, and half wits abound.
Few like thy genius at proportions aim,
All great, all graceful and throughout the same.

Such be thy life, since the glorious Rage
That fir'd thy youth flames unsubdued by age,
Though wealth nor fame now touch thy sated mind
Still tinge the canvas, bounteous to mankind.
Since after thee may rise an impious line,
Coarse manglers of the human face divine,
Paint on till fate dissolve thy mortal part,
And live and die the monarch of thy art.'

Richard Steele too wrote a poem on the same subject. Tickell combined friendship with the political animosity which led to the Addison-Pope feud. The participants flitted in and out of Kneller's town or country house as it might happen.

Alexander Pope, though still very young, had already made a name for himself, and his *Essay on Criticism* had received favourable comment from Addison in No. 253 of the *Spectator*. Pope was a Catholic who modelled himself on John Dryden, and added to this, a sense of inferiority caused by his deformity and small stature had already made him very susceptible to criticism. In 1715 he, being then twenty-seven years old, produced the first volume of his translation of Homer's *Iliad*; no sooner had it appeared than another translation came from the pen of Thomas Tickell. Tickell in his preface disclaimed all rivalry to Pope, but the simultaneous appearance of these books could only lead to trouble and Addison appears to have said that Tickell's translation was more faithful and better than Pope's. This may well have been the truth, for Pope was no great scholar and he worked from previous translations, whilst Tickell was a scholar and as Addison's Secretary doubtless had Addison's assistance in the work. Pope's friend John Gay did not help matters by going to him and saying: 'I am told at Buttons your character is made free with as to morals and that Mr. Addison says your translation and Tickell's are both well done but that the latter has more of Homer.'

Unfortunately Pope considered that he would stand or fall by his Homer and money was important to him. He bore no malice towards Tickell, but great hatred towards Addison, with whom he was quite out of sympathy. The breach widened and Pope then began the attack which culminated in his satire on

72. ALEXANDER POPE

Engraved by John Faber, Junior (1738)

73. WILLIAM CONGREVE (1709)

National Portrait Gallery (Kit Kat Collection)

Addison as Atticus; the seeds of the quarrel can be traced to Pope's inferiority complex, rivalry and the dislike of criticism, and they were well fertilized by political animosity, though the Tories had by then been defeated by the arrival of the Hanoverian monarch.

But before going into detail on the relationship of Kneller with Pope, who was nearly fifty years his junior, we had best turn to the right-wing or Tory writers with whom Kneller was friendly and in close contact.

Jonathan Swift (1667-1745) came over to London in 1708 from Dublin, where he was Rector of Agher in County Meath, to see Godolphin and his ministry about the claims of the Protestant clergy in Ireland. We find in his *Journal to Stella*, which he wrote from 1710 to 1713 when chiefly in London or on his way to or from Ireland, reference to Godfrey Kneller.

On October 5th, 1710, for instance, he writes:

'This morning Delaval came to see me, and we went to Kneller's, who was not in town.'

There are further entries:

'December 6th, 1710.

. . . Congreve and Delaval have at last prevailed on Sir Godfrey Kneller to entreat me to let him draw my picture for nothing. I know not when I shall sit. . . .'

'February 8th, 1712.

. . . Lady Orkney has given me her picture; a very fine original of Sir Godfrey Kneller's; it is now amending. He has favoured her squint admirably; and you know I love a cast in the eye. . . .'

'February 27th, 1712.

. . . Did I tell you that I have a very fine picture of Lady Orkney, an original, by Sir Godfrey Kneller, three-quarter-length; I have it now at home with a very fine frame. . . .'

Swift had already remarked on Lady Orkney's squint, for he humorously wrote:

'Lady Orkney is making me a writing table of her own contrivance and a bed nightgown. She is perfectly kind like a mother. I think the devil was in it the other day that I should talk of that ugly squinting cousin of hers, and the poor lady herself, you know, squints like a dragon.'

Perhaps Godfrey knew of this when he emphasized the squint.

Congreve was a schoolfellow of Swift at Kilkenny, and the two Irishmen, though they were to diverge on political opinion, remained good friends. In his early days Swift was a Whig, and in 1701, a few months after he had taken his Doctorate of Divinity, he published *The Discourse on the Dissensions in Athens and Rome*, which was attributed at first to Somers or Burnett. When he came over in 1701 to claim for the Clergy the first-fruits and twentieth now known as Queen Anne's Bounty he cannot yet have left the Whigs, or at any rate have been out of favour, for he was selected by the hierarchy and clergy of Ireland to represent them. By 1710 he had gone over to the Tories and was writing for the Tory *Examiner*.

When in London, Swift saw a good deal of Kneller, but he returned to Dublin in 1713 as Dean of St. Patrick's and except for visits remained there. Kneller never painted him, and the best pictures of the Dean are by the Irish-born artist Charles Jervas, to whom he sat both in London and Dublin, and by Francis Bindon at Howth Castle. In Dublin, Jervas also painted Esther Johnson, his Stella, and the pictures are now in the Dublin National Gallery. It is of interest to note that Swift through his mother was a kinsman of Kneller's early friend John Dryden.

Two other Tory friends of Kneller's were Matthew Prior, who complimented Kneller on his picture of the Duke of Ormonde, and Dr. John Arbuthnot (1667-1735), the physician and author who used to meet Swift and Pope in the Scriblerus Club where bad and artificial contemporary writing was debunked.

Matthew Prior, of whom there is a very fine portrait by Kneller at Trinity College, Cambridge, was the Editor of the Tory *Examiner* and had produced the *Town and Country Mouse* with Halifax in reply to Dryden's *Hind and the Panther*.

A mutual friend of Kneller's and Pope's was John Gay (1685-1732), now best remembered as the author later of the *Beggar's Opera*. John Gay had written a poem entitled *Mr. Pope's Welcome from Greece*, of which one of the verses reads,

> 'Kneller amid the triumph bears his part
> Who could, were mankind lost, anew create
> What can the extent of his vast soul confine?
> A painter, critic, engineer, divine.'

One day Gay (74) was reading a poem to Kneller which contained much flattery; it may indeed have been the above verse. Gay thought he had pushed the flattery a little too far and that Godfrey Kneller would think himself too bantered. On asking his opinion Godfrey replied with his guttural accent:

'Ay, Mr. Gay, all what you have said is very fine and very true; but you have forgotten one thing, my good friend, by God I should have been the general of an army for when I was in Venice there was a Girandole (display of fireworks) and all the Palace St. Mark was in smoke of gunpowder and I did like the smell, Mr. Gay; I should have been a great general, Mr. Gay.'

This is another insight into Kneller's vanity, but so gross is it that one can but believe that he said it with a twinkle.

Alexander Pope's friendship ripened during the last ten years of Godfrey's life. We know that Pope took painting lessons from Kneller's old pupil Jervas in 1713, and it was about this time that Kneller and Pope began a long and intermittent correspondence which culminated in a family row over the memorial in Twickenham Church. Though a pupil of Jervas, Pope used to copy Kneller's works. Lord Mansfield has a picture of Betterton the actor by Pope after Kneller, though Pope laid no great claim to his own skill.

The Pope-Kneller correspondence throws an interesting light on the latter's character, and proves that he was not an unbusinesslike man, though at the same time the young Pope was well able to pull his leg.

The correspondence is based on two things. First, Pope was anxious to obtain and furnish a house for the Wortley Montagus at Twickenham, where both Pope and Kneller were living in 1719; further, Pope wished Kneller to paint Lady Mary Wortley Montagu. The great lady, an attractive but pedantic blue-stocking, was born in 1689, being the daughter of the 1st Duke of Kingston and his wife Lady Mary Feilding, daughter of William, Earl of Denbigh. Her sisters were Frances, Lady Mar, whom Kneller painted in 1715, and Lady Gower. She is said to have been brought to the Kit Kat Club to be toasted by her father, she says 'when not eight years old.'

The letter of 16th June 1719 from Great Queen Street reads:

'SIR,—I am in towne, and have louck'd for beds and bedsteads which must cost ten pounds a year. When I promised to provide them you made no mention of towne rate, which I am to pay, and will be 5 pounds a year at least, which would be fifteen pounds per annum with the beds, and that house did let for forty-five years when I bought it, so that all I have laid out being nearly 400 pounds, would be done for nothing, of which you will consider and let me know your mind. The stables are fitted as your gentleman ordered them to be, and all the painting will be done to-morrow or Thursday with wainscoating in the quickest manner and best; and if you can stay till Saturday let me know your pleasure about the beds and bedsteads for them I cannot provide. You may have 6 of which two are to have coirtins for ten pounds a year and I am giving my most humble respects to Lady Mary Wortley.—Yours,
G. KNELLER.

I thought one might have had such beds and bedsteads for 4 or 5 pounds a year.'

Anyhow, a deal was made, beds or no beds, and the Wortley Montagus moved into a house on Kneller's Twickenham estate.

Pope revealed to Kneller in a letter full of flattery, which read:

'. . . Whatever another man can be, a wise and great painter, at least, can be above the stars when he pleases. The elevation of such a genius is not to be measured by the object it flies at; it soars rather higher than its aim and carries up the subject along with it. . . .

I thought to compliment upon paper had been left to the poet and lovers. Dryden says he had seen a fool think in your picture of him. And I have no reason to say that I have seen the least of mankind appear one of the greatest under your hands.'

Godfrey Kneller painted three chiaroscuro pictures from the statues of Apollo, Venus and Hercules for Pope's Villa at Twickenham.

These pictures were left by Pope to Lord Bathurst and now hang at Cirencester; they were paid for with the following lines:

'What God, what genius did the pencil move,
When Kneller painted these:
'Twas friendship, warm as Phoebus, kind as love,
And strong as Hercules.'

And Godfrey Kneller wrote in reply:

'DEAR FRIEND,—I find them pictures are so fresh being painted in three collers, and ought to be near the flier for several days for as they are it is impracticable to put them where you intend. It would be a pitty, that they should take dust. Jenny stays here eight to ten days and I will not fail of sending them when reddy and I am giving my heart and humble servis to your dear mother, Mr. Pope.'

There are two rather amusing notes from Kneller to Pope which give a sidelight on the society of the day.

One reads:

'DEAR MR. POPE,—I believe this will be a card players' evening and we may do as we please. If you come about four o'clock you may see me paint. To-morrow I am engaged to go to Harrow-on-the-Hill with company being ever dear friend. . . .'

The other, at a later date, deals with his health, for he wrote to Pope:

'I hope your genus dos and will know myn is with most acceptable and most accomplished company to-morrow; for my body is in no condition to stir out of bed as yet and has had no rest these two nights but what it snatches and gets in the day time by fits; and I believe my leg will be out of order a good while.

Pray give my heart good will. . . .'

In the meanwhile Godfrey had painted Lady Mary Wortley Montagu. The first we hear of it is in a letter from Pope to her. It is undated but would appear to be shortly after the house transaction.

'*Sunday.*

Indeed, dear madam, it is not possible to tell you whether you give me everyday I see you more pleasure or more respect. And upon my word, whenever I see you after a day or twos absence, it is in just such a view as that you yesterday had of your own writings. I find you still better than I could imagine. I think I was impartial before to your prejudice.

The picture dwells really at my heart and I have had a perfect passion of preferring your present face to your past. I know and thoroughly esteem yourself of this year. I know no more of Lady Mary Pierrepoint than to admire at what I have heard from her, or be pleased with some fragments of hers as I am with Sapphos. But now I cannot say what I would say of you now. Only still give me cause to say you are good to me, and allow me as much of your person as Sir Godfrey can help me to. Upon conferring with him yesterday I find he thinks it absolutely necessary to draw the face first, which he says can never be set right on the figure of the drapery or the posture be finished before. To give you as little trouble as possible, he proposed to draw your face with crayons, and finish it up at your own house, in a morning; from whence he will transfer it to the canvas, so that you need not go sit at his house. This, I must observe, is a manner in which they seldom draw any but crowned heads; and I observe it with secret pride and pleasure.

Be so kind as to tell me, if you care he should do this tomorrow at twelve. Though I am but assured from you of the thing let the manner and time be what you best like. I should be very unworthy of any favour from your hands, if I desired any at the expense of your quiet or conveniency in any degree.

I have just received this pamphlet. . . .'

74. JOHN GAY

National Portrait Gallery

75. PETER THE GREAT (1697)

H.M. The King, Kensington Palace

This was followed by two further letters. The first read:

'MADAM,—Sir G. happening to come from London yesterday (as I did myself) will wait upon you this morning at twelve, to take a sketch of you in your dress if you will give me leave. He is really very good to me. I heartily hope you will be in so too. But I submit to you in all things; nay in the manner of all things, your own pleasure and your own time. Upon my word I will take you and understand you as will be understood, with a real respect and resignation when you are doing me anything. Yours will be done; but God send it may be the same with mine.

I beg a single word, in answer, because I am to see Sir Godfrey accordingly.'

And the second:

'MADAM,—Yours received, I suppose the epistle Sir G. dictated to me which abating a few flowers was word for word. My concern that you should be settled in the neighbourhood has since put me on further enquiries and I find there is a pretty good house in the town opposite that which my Lord William Pawlett has taken.'

Kneller completed the picture to Pope's extreme satisfaction. I am not certain of its whereabouts to-day, but of it Pope wrote:

'*Extemporaneous Lines on the Picture of Lady Mary Wortley Montagu
by Kneller*

The playful smiles around the dimpled mouth,
That happy air of majesty and truth;
So would I draw (but oh! tis vain to try,
My narrow genius does the power deny)
The equal lustre of the heavenly mind,
Where every grace with every virtue's joined;
Learning not vain, and wisdom not severe,
With greatness easy and with wit sincere;
With just description show the work divine,
And the whole princess in my work should shine.'

So Godfrey Kneller lived with and through the literary world from Catholic Dryden to Catholic Pope, holding in his studio and drawing-room the balance of power, as perhaps only an atheist and foreigner could do amid the bitter factions which arose through the new succession to the monarchy.

CHAPTER X

THE KIT KAT CLUB

TOWARDS the end of the seventeenth century the leading Whigs, noblemen, writers and members of Parliament, used to meet in a tavern near Temple Bar owned by one Christopher Kat. Over a bottle of wine and one of Kat's good mutton pies, known as Kit Kats, they discussed the politics of the day—which centred, as all politics did, on the Revolution Settlement and the succession of the House of Hanover. In between the discussions a lady of fashion, more often than not a daughter or wife of one of the family, might be brought along and toasted; the names of those toasted are remembered by glasses on which their names were engraved or by the toast lists which still exist. One of the earliest women to be toasted was Lady Mary Pierrepoint, who, as we have seen, was taken by her father the Duke of Kingston—which would have been when the Club was just starting. Another, and perhaps the most popular toast (for she appears often on the list), was Lady Anne Churchill, the Duke of Marlborough's daughter who married Lord Sunderland and was known as 'Little Whig.'

In 1703 Jacob Tonson (77), the publisher who had become secretary of the Club, built a room adjoining his house at Barn Elms where the members were to meet. The Duke of Somerset decided to commission Godfrey Kneller to paint all the members for Tonson. The earliest date on pictures is 1705, but some may well have been painted two years earlier.

The pictures were painted on canvases 36″ by 27″ and were designed to hang in two rows in Tonson's room. This size enabled Kneller to show his skill by including one or two hands in what was a short half-length. The phrase Kit Kat is now used for any short half-length showing one or two hands on any size canvas and also on any size plate in photography.

The principles of the Club were, first, religious toleration (toleration, that is, of all but Roman Catholics), the defence of the Settlement, the cause of the Hanoverian succession, and in order to implement these three causes the further-ance of the prosecution of the war against France which supported the Pretender and the Stuart claims.

Kneller was not a member for he was no politician. He belonged to clubs which were purely social such as—The Social Club! A circular exists which announces that this club was to be revived in 1706; the list of members reads:

'The Honble. Order of Little Bedlam and the list of members and their names in the Club:

The Great Master John Earl of Exeter	Lyon
William Duke of Devonshire	Leopard
Earl of Denbigh	Tyger
Ant. Verrio	Porcupine
Sir Godfrey Kneller	Unicorne'

Godfrey enjoyed the social side of the Kit Kat Club. As he painted all the members he was often invited to dine with them, and his own portrait, almost in miniature, was included in the collection.

The last picture is dated 1717, about the time that the Club ceased to exist, although the series may have been completed up to 1720. In 1725 we find Sir John Vanbrugh, one of the members, bemoaning its disappearance in a letter to Jacob Tonson, writing of memories of the Club as a thing of the past. He suggested a further meeting 'not as a club but old friends that have been of a club, and the best club that ever met.'

Between the years 1703 and 1717 (it may have met as late as 1720) the meetings took place at Barn Elms, but often, probably when Parliament was sitting, they would drive out nearer to London, to the Flask Inn in Hampstead.

The Kit Kat collection of portraits represents 43 members on 42 canvases, for the Duke of Newcastle and his brother-in-law the 7th Earl of Lincoln share a canvas (58). They are seated at a table facing each other and drinking—a very attractive portrait conversation piece, and the only one not conforming to the Kit Kat size, because it was designed to hang over the chimney-piece at Barn Elms.

In 1725 John Faber Junior engraved and published the complete set of Kit Kat pictures. The folio is dedicated to Charles, Duke of Somerset. The dedication reads:

> 'As this collection of prints owes its very being to your Grace's liberality, in setting the example to the members of the Kit Kat Club of honouring Mr. Tonson with their picture ...'

In Faber's series there are four mezzotint pictures not now with the collection, and the fact has been taken to indicate that four are missing. They are those of the Duke of Marlborough, Edward Hopkins and Lords Huntingdon and Burlington. Edward Hopkins and Huntingdon are shown only by heads in the rough *pentimento* of the rest of the picture, in the same way as the Viscount Shannon which hangs with the collection to-day.

The first assumption would be that these pictures are missing, and a letter from Henrietta, Countess of Godolphin, who had succeeded her father in 1722 as Duchess of Marlborough in her own right, which was reproduced in *Country Life* on 24th June 1925, would further bear out this view. This letter, addressed to Jacob Tonson Junior, reads:

> 'SIR,—I know 'tis only the set of these Pictures that your Uncle value and not that which I would give the world for, therefore sure except 'tis purely out of the ill nature and having no respect for that Picture he would change with me for an Original one, of Sir Godfrey Kneller just the same size of the Kit Kat ones, wish this was in your power.
>
> I am your humble servant,
>
> MARLBOROUGH.

November 29th (1729).'

No further correspondence has been traced, and on first reading the letter it might be assumed that this picture referred to the 'Missing' painting of the late Duke of Marlborough himself. But it is known that Henrietta loved William Congreve and was responsible after his death in 1729 for the erection of his monument in Westminster Abbey. The effigy on this monument is a sculptured reproduction of the Kit Kat picture by Kneller, and it may well be that Henrietta, Duchess of Marlborough, was trying to obtain this picture (73 and 76) for herself, for except in Faber's series there is no other reference to a portrait of Marlborough.

It will be noticed in Faber's Folio that the plates of Marlborough, Edward Hopkins and Burlington are not numbered through in accordance with the series, but Marlborough is shown as between 5 and 6, Burlington between 15 and 16, Edward Hopkins between 41 and 42. Strangely enough, we find Huntingdon numbered as 12, but Dartiquenave the epicure and wit is placed between 40 and 41. The natural inference is that the four 'missing' pictures were not at the time with the collection, or in fact ever were with it, but that Somerset knew these subjects had been members of the Club and wished them to be included. There may have been an intention of including them, but they never formed part of the collection of portraits when housed by Tonson at Barn Elms. In the early part of the last century the missing Dartiquenave was replaced by a copy and the National Portrait Gallery have recently found the original, though it has not been cut down to Kit Kat size. It is not at present hanging in the National Portrait Gallery with the Kit Kat series.

If there is a missing Kit Kat it is that of Huntingdon. But the others never formed part of the collection and the picture of Charles Dartiquenave would appear to have been added.

The Director of the National Portrait Gallery kindly let me look through the various papers he obtained when the Kit Kat pictures were presented to the Nation by the National Art Collection fund in 1944. Among them I found a diagram and key. I found from this list that Marlborough, Huntingdon, Edward Hopkins, Burlington, Dartiquenave and Dunch were missing. It is difficult to date this diagram. If it is a diagram of Barn Elms, which I don't believe it to be from the shape, then it answers our problem. We know that Dunch was missing for many years, having been lent to Sir Henry Oxenden to be copied, and was only returned in 1814. I think the diagram shows one of the later eighteenth-century resting-places of the pictures.

Comparing Faber's mezzotints with the present collection, one also notices that William Walsh is shown by Faber as an unfinished picture in 1735; it is now finished and therefore the coat and body must have been painted in at a later date.

A letter from Congreve to Jacob Tonson, dated 1695, would give the impression that the Club was in being and the picture of Congreve painted as early as that year.

The letter, which is dated 20th August, reads:

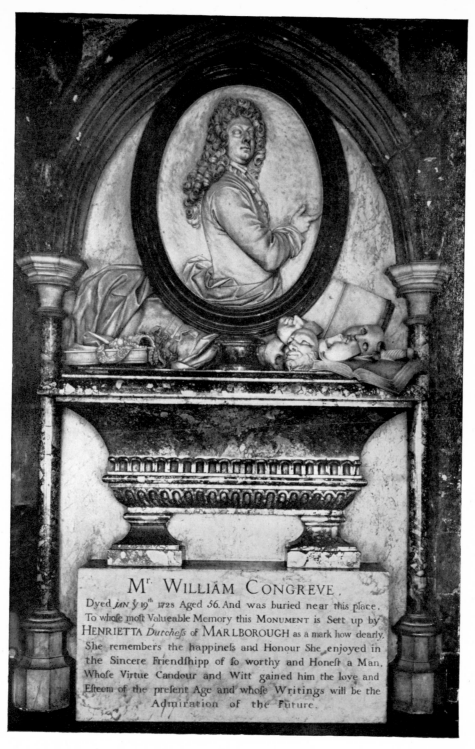

Mr. WILLIAM CONGREVE,
Dyed *Jan* y 19th 1728 Aged 56. And was buried near this place.
To whose most Valueable Memory this MONUMENT is Sett up by
HENRIETTA *Dutchess* of MARLBOROUGH as a mark how dearly.
She remembers the happiness and Honour She enjoyed in
the Sincere Friendshipp of so worthy and Honest a Man,
Whose Virtue Candour and Witt gained him the love and
Esteem of the present Age and whose Writings will be the
Admiration of the Future.

76. MONUMENT TO CONGREVE IN WESTMINSTER ABBEY

The portrait medallion was carved by Francis Bird after the portrait
by Kneller (*cf.* Plate 73)

77. JACOB TONSON (1717)

National Portrait Gallery (Kit Kat Collection)

'I am glad that you approve so much of my picture. If you should see Sir Godfrey again before you go out of town pray give him my service, but if he has not finish'd the picture give him a hint for I should be glad were it done before my return.'

This does not, I think, refer to the Kit Kat *Congreve* which is dated 1709, or to the excellent portrait which hangs in the Senate House at Trinity College, Dublin, which shows Congreve an older man.

After the Club closed, the pictures remained at Barn Elms and in 1736 Jacob Tonson died in Herefordshire. The pictures then passed to his nephew Jacob 2, and his great-nephew Jacob 3. It appears he moved them to a house near Ditton, where they were reputed to be hanging in the middle of the eighteenth century. On Jacob 3's death the pictures passed to his brother Richard Tonson, M.P. for Windsor, who lived at Down Place near Water Oakley. The pictures were removed there and a room was built for them about the next year (perhaps the room in the Diagram). They were only at Down Place until 1772, when Richard died and the pictures passed to his sister, Lady Mary Baker, the widow of Sir William Baker. It appears that the pictures were housed by her son Simon Baker at Bayfordbury and on Simon's death they passed to his brother in 1840. In 1812 they had been housed in a special room built by the Bakers at Bayfordbury, and there they remained until 1945.

There is an amusing account in Sir Richard Phillips's *A Morning's Walk from London to Kew*, published in London in 1820. Phillips found the ruins of the old gallery at Barn Elms and wrote:

'The entire building for want of ventilation having become a food for fungus, called dry rot, the timber had lost its cohesive powers . . . here I found the Kit Kat room nearly as it existed in its glory. It is eighteen feet high and forty feet long by twenty wide. The mouldings and ornaments were in the most superb fashion of its age: but the whole was falling to pieces from the effects of dry rot.

My attention was chiefly attracted by the faded cloth hanging on the room, whose red colour once set off the famous portraits of the club, that hung around it. Their marks and sizes were still visible, and the numbers remained as written in chalk for the guidance of the hanger. . . . I read their names aloud.'

Alas, when he read their names aloud he did not make a note which would help us to know how they were hung and so solve the mystery of the missing pictures.

It appears that Godfrey was a little slipshod and careless in his commission. I discuss the merits of the various pictures later; but from contemporary accounts he appears perhaps to have skimped them a little. There is an amusing account from Vanbrugh to Tonson, then on the Continent, dated 15th June 1703:

'In short the Kit Kat wants you much more than you want them. Those who remain in town are in great desire of waiting on you at Barn Elms, not that they have finished the picture either, tho' to excuse (as well as myself) Sir Godfrey has been most at fault. The fool has a country house near Hampton Court and is so busy about fitting it up to receive (nobody) that there is no getting him to work.'

N

This letter shows that the first members were being painted in this year. The house at Hampton Court was not that near Twickenham which Kneller was to go to ten years later, but probably some smaller house he had taken for the summer to be near his friend Sir Christopher Wren, who was working down there when not living opposite St. Paul's on Cardinal's Wharf.

This Kit Kat collection shows and portrays all the eminent Whigs—in fact, all those in power—at the beginning of the eighteenth century.

There is a very good little brochure prepared by the National Portrait Gallery with notes by Miss Mary Ransome which can be obtained by those who want further details.

Of the forty-three members whom we have in the collection, not more than thirty probably were members at the same time—for instance, the Earl of Dorset died in 1706, George Stepney in 1707, William Walsh in 1708, Lord Essex in 1710, Arthur Maynwaring in 1712, and Lord Carbery and John Tidcombe in 1713, whilst it is unlikely that the Dukes of Newcastle, Grafton, Dorset and Montagu or Lords Lincoln, Berkeley, Scarborough and Bath joined before 1713.

The pictures can be roughly divided into the nine Dukes, the nineteen noblemen including courtiers, politicians and soldiers, the seven authors and eight diplomats, country squires and gentlemen at large.

The father of the Club was Charles Sackville, 6th Earl of Dorset (1638-1706), courtier and poet. He was older by a year than John Vaughan, 3rd Earl of Carbery (1639-1713), who succeeded Lord Dorset on his death as senior member. Carbery was in his turn succeeded by John Somers, Baron Somers (1650-1716), as probably the oldest and senior member.

The nine Dukes who formed part of the Club were: Charles Montagu, 1st Duke of Manchester (1662-1722), who must not be confused with John Montagu, 2nd Duke of Montagu (1688-1749), both of whom were members. The other Dukes were Thomas Pelham-Holles, 1st Duke of Newcastle (1693-1768); Charles Lennox, 1st Duke of Richmond (1672-1723); Charles Fitzroy, 2nd Duke of Grafton (1683-1752); Lionel Sackville, 1st Duke of Dorset (1688-1765); William Cavendish, 2nd Duke of Devonshire (1673-1729); Evelyn Pierrepoint, 1st Duke of Kingston (1665-1726); and Charles Seymour, 6th Duke of Somerset (1662-1748).

Manchester was a diplomat and soldier who had been Ambassador at Venice, Vienna and Paris and had fought at the Battle of the Boyne; he is represented in a full-length wig and blue coat, and his is probably one of the earliest pictures. Manchester's kinsman, Montagu, served in France during the life of the Club and probably retailed stories of his adventures as soldier. He married Marlborough's youngest daughter. Besides being a soldier we also find that he was a Fellow of the Royal College of Surgeons and of the Royal Society, and an early Grand Master of the Grand Lodge of English Freemasons.

Newcastle, who, as we have said, is shown on the same canvas as his brother-in-law Lincoln, was a politician. A staunch Hanoverian, he was to come very much to the political forefront after the accession of George I and the winding up of the Club. He was Prime Minister between 1754 and 1756, and again from 1757 to 1762, important years in English colonial development; his absurdities are chronicled by Smollett.

Richmond, a son of Charles II and the Duchess of Portsmouth, had gone into exile with James II, but returned to England in 1692 and threw in his lot with the Established Church and the Williamites.

Grafton—a sickly-looking youth painted wearing a head turban (34)—was likewise descended from Charles II, being a grandson of Barbara, Duchess of Cleveland, whom Kneller painted. Grafton cut no political figure, being a fox-hunting and supposedly witty courtier.

Dorset was the son of Charles, Earl of Dorset, father of the Club; he was certainly not a member of the Club until after his father's death and was to be a courtier to George I and George II.

Devonshire had been an M.P., as had Lady Mary Wortley Montagu's father, Kingston. An original member of the Club, he was later to become Lord President of the Council under George I. Whilst Lord Dorset was the 'father,' the Duke of Somerset was probably the originator of the Club and certainly, as Faber's dedication to the engraving shows, started the idea of painting the members' portraits for Tonson. He was very pompous and known as the 'Proud Duke.' This is noticeable in the haughty glance of his eyes in Kneller's portrait, which is in full-length wig and brown drapery; strangely enough, despite Somerset's patronage of the portraits, his own is not one of the best in the collection.

The other noblemen were Charles, 6th Earl of Dorset (1638-1706); Charles Montagu, 1st Earl of Halifax (1661-1715); and Henry Clinton, 7th Earl of Lincoln, whom we have mentioned; Thomas Wharton, 1st Marquess of Wharton (1648-1716); Charles Mohun, 4th Baron Mohun (1677-1712); Richard Temple, 1st Viscount Cobham (1675-1749); Charles Howard, 3rd Earl of Carlisle (1669-1738); James Berkeley, 3rd Earl of Berkeley (1680-1736); Francis Godolphin, 2nd Earl of Godolphin (1678-1766); Richard Boyle, Viscount Shannon (1675-1740); John Vaughan, 3rd Earl of Carbery (1639-1713); James Stanhope, 1st Earl Stanhope (1674-1721); Robert Walpole, 1st Earl of Orford (1676-1745); Spencer Compton, Earl of Wilmington (1674-1743); John Somers, Baron Somers (1651-1716); Richard Lumley, 2nd Earl of Scarborough (1688-1740); William Pulteney, Earl of Bath (1684-1764); Algernon Capell, 2nd Earl of Essex (1670-1726); and Charles, 4th Baron Cornwallis (1675-1722).

Of these noblemen Mohun, Cobham, Shannon, Stanhope, Scarborough and Essex were soldiers and Berkeley a sailor. Mohun was a notorious rake and duellist. He rose to the rank of general under Marlborough, but was killed in the duel with the Duke of Hamilton commemorated in *Esmond*, when both participants died. Cobham rose to the rank of field-marshal, and to him we owe the rebuilding of Stowe, near Buckingham (now a public school).

Shannon, who is only shown by his head, the picture being unfinished, also rose to the rank of field-marshal, and was commemorated as a soldier by Roubiliac at Walton-on-Thames.

Essex was a brother-in-law to Carlisle, the courtier, who, like Cobham, was a great patron of Vanbrugh, who built Castle Howard for him. Thus to the Kit Kat Club we may owe Stowe, Castle Howard and Woodstock.

Godolphin was the son of Queen Anne's chief minister and had formerly been a moderate Tory. According to Chesterfield he always slept in the House of Lords, and as he was so stupid it did not matter on which side he slept. He is best remembered to-day as the owner of the famous 'Godolphin Arabian Sire.'

Halifax was the patron and collaborator with Prior in the *Town and Country Mouse*, and organized within the Club a subscription to encourage good comedies. We do not know the outcome, but £300 was collected for this purpose.

Carbery had been an early patron of Dryden's before the latter changed his views. Some books say that a portrait of Dryden hung with the Kit Kat pictures as part of the collection; this was politically impossible, though the Baker family did own a portrait of Dryden and hung it in the same room. This portrait is now in the National Portrait Gallery. Walpole was Prime Minister from 1720 to 1742, and among his great art collection were many of the Knellers which passed in due course to Horace Walpole; those that were not sold at the Strawberry Hill Sale in the last century are now at Houghton.

Somers, a lawyer, had defended Seven Bishops who had opposed James II, and was President of the Royal Society from 1698 to 1703. Another portrait of his hangs at Burlingham House. Cornwallis was a politician.

We have written of the authors in the previous chapter. They included Congreve, Steele, Joseph Addison (1672-1719), Sir Samuel Garth, also a physician of great repute and a friend of Dryden and Pope, Sir John Vanbrugh, architect and playwright, Arthur Maynwaring (1668-1712) and William Walsh (1663-1708). Maynwaring had been a Jacobite, but later edited the Whig *Examiner*; William Walsh, though a critic and poet, was more of a dilettante and wit, and is best remembered as the early friend and patron of Pope.

The series is completed by Abraham Stanyan (1669-1732) and George Stepney (1663-1707), both diplomats; Edmund Dunch (1657-1719) and John (later Lord) Dormer (1691-1785), both country gentlemen. The former was an M.P., and little is known of the latter. Charles Dartiquenave (1664-1737) was a wit and epicure who contributed to the *Tatler* (79), whilst John Tidcombe (1642-1713), a very early member of the Club, was a soldier. This leaves us with Jacob Tonson (1656-1736), the publisher and bookseller, who was the Club's secretary and for whom the paintings were made, and lastly, but of some importance perhaps to some members, Thomas Hopkins, a moneylender, who died in 1720.

The pictures, except those of Grafton and Tonson, which are in turbans, and Shannon, which is unfinished, are in wigs—full-length wigs, in most cases—but

78. VISCOUNT SHANNON (1717)

National Portrait Gallery (Kit Kat Collection)

80. LORD MOHUN

Engraved by John Faber, Junior (1732)

79. CHARLES DARTIQUENAVE

Engraved by John Faber, Junior (1734)

despite this similarity of head-dress and attire the characters are mostly well painted and the 42 canvases in the same limited space are not overpowering.

In Congreve (73) we can see the vain but witty type, in Steele (47) the Irish character and humour, and in Mohun the rakishness of the man (80). The last named forced his way into the Club despite opposition from Tonson, and the first night disgraced himself by breaking off the gilt ornaments from the back of chairs. Kneller represents him with a locket, doubtless of some actress or light lady, and gives him a streak of coarseness and sensuality; Kneller, like Tonson, disliked Mohun.

There is an account of this episode in Spence's *Anecdotes*, of how Lord Mohun on the day that he was elected broke the gold emblem on his chair. It appears that he was going to be mimicked or laughed at, and did not care for the prospect. Tonson is reputed to have said that a man who did that would cut another man's throat.

A half-hour spent with the Kit Kat pictures—which is now possible to all visitors in London, whilst most museums have the Faber Folio—gives a great insight into the early years of the eighteenth century. At the same time the majority of pictures show Kneller at his best. At the beginning of the century he was painting people whom he liked and knew. He portrayed their likeness and characters well despite the criticism of shoddiness so often cast at him.

CHAPTER XI

THE LAST YEARS—1702-1723

IN 1702 Godfrey Kneller's brother John Zachary died in London. It was about this time that we ceased tracing Godfrey's life in England so that we might review his work, his assistants and his friends, and it is time now to take up again the direct narrative of his life.

He was still living at Covent Garden at this time, one of his neighbours being the eminent Dr. Radcliffe. The Doctor's house was in Bow Street, whilst Kneller's was in the north-east corner of the garden in the Piazza near the entrance to Covent Garden Theatre. They had a common boundary wall, and as the two were good friends the pass door was kept open. Kneller, besides his love of painting and music, was also very fond of flowers and kept his garden in London in great order; but one day, looking out of the window, he saw Radcliffe's servants picking the flowers in his garden, so he summoned the servants to take word to their master that he must close the door.

Radcliffe, as happens if others accuse one's servants of anything out of place, was rather peevish, and replied by sending word to Godfrey that he could do anything he liked with the door but paint it. To which Godfrey briskly replied: 'and I can take anything from the doctor but his physic.'

But the house in the Piazza was getting too small now that the number of Kneller's assistants and pupils had grown. About 1703 we find that he was looking for a house elsewhere, and he bought 55 and 56 besides 57 and 58 Great Queen Street, which runs out of Lincoln's Inn Fields. It was whilst he was moving from one to the other that he took the house near Hampton Court which Vanbrugh had mentioned in his letter to Tonson. It was a busy time for Godfrey, for he was at work on the early Kit Kat pictures, besides being commissioned by the new Queen for many special tasks. The first had been to design the Coronation medal. Godfrey drew Queen Anne for this and on the reverse had made a representation of the Goddess Pallas destroying a Giant, as we find from *The Postman* of 2/4 April 1702. Bird modelled the medal but the Queen did not like it and asked whether Rotier could not make a design. She was told Rotier had left England, but Godfrey found that the old engraver was still in the country. Rotier was angry, probably because he had not been approached first of all; although he started off on the medal he died before it was finished. Then in 1703 Godfrey was commissioned also by the Queen to paint the Emperor Charles VI at Portsmouth; this he did, but Walpole rather scathingly says in comparing it with the

Peter the Great that Kneller must have 'felt the fall from Peter to Charles.' Then, besides the Kit Kat pictures, he was completing the *Admirals* which then were to hang in Thornhill's Painted Hall at Greenwich.

Despite the commissions for the Kit Kat and Admiral series, besides medals and private commissions and house moving, Godfrey Kneller decided to marry. His wife was Mrs. Susannah Graves, a widow, and they were married at St. Bride's Church on 23rd January 1703. Lady Kneller was the daughter of the Rev. John Cawley, Archdeacon of Lincoln and Rector of Henley-on-Thames. Her grandfather was William Cawley, a well-known regicide.

She must have been a very broad-minded woman and may well have been nearly his age, for she does not appear to have felt strongly his association with Mrs. Voss, and her daughter Agnes was accepted in the house. Certainly there were no children of the marriage, but Kneller painted a fine noble picture of her. The Rev. John Cawley is buried in the Parish Church at Henley-on-Thames, where he died on 13th August 1709.

A few years afterwards Agnes Voss married one Huckle and in 1710 they had a son. Kneller requested that he should be godfather to this child, whom he adopted and who in 1731—on attaining his majority—was to take the name of Kneller.

Little is known of Lady Kneller until after his death, but it appears that she kept in the background, just running the house for him.

Godfrey was to live in Great Queen Street until he died. It was to this house that Steele and Addison, Pope, Prior, Gay and Congreve were to come to gossip with him, besides the many men and women who came in the first two decades of the eighteenth century to be painted.

During this time Kneller was a member of St. Luke's Club, a circle of painters of which Van Dyck and Lely had been members. The painters had discussed the question of an Academy, and in 1697 it had almost been started. However, the Academy to which Highmore went was opened under Kneller's auspices in 1711, but certain forms and ceremonies were introduced into it which some members did not like. Pupils, teachers and directors were at odds among themselves. Kneller found he was being mimicked and laughed at, and he finally resigned and closed the doors, which were not to reopen until Vanderbank's time a few years later.

Kneller by now was making a comfortable fortune and decided to buy a country house; he found a site at Whitton near Twickenham, and in 1709 he began to build a large house which was completed in 1711 (82). The house was very stately and of the period. It was over the decorating of this house that Kneller had his quarrel with Thornhill, whom he had employed to decorate the stairs, as previously recounted. It will be remembered that he found Thornhill was painting Isaac Newton, whom Kneller had painted in 1702.

Though he worked in London, Kneller would spend the summer months at Whitton. Here he had many friends, including Pope, who came to Twickenham in 1715. Berkeley, Stafford, Wharton, and many other noblemen also lived there. He did the house up very sumptuously, and we find that George Vertue in one of his Notebooks remarked on the fine collection of pictures which included:

> 'At Whitton House,
>> Done at Rome—a piece of the Roman Amphitheatre dated 1677 (J. Kneller and G. Kneller)
>>> $\frac{1}{2}$ l of a man in chair—Rubens
>
> A head of Rembrandt
> a man $\frac{1}{2}$ l—Van D
> Of men two heads ovals
> 12 small copies of beauties of HC
> The staircase painted by Laguerre which a fine design represents the arts—cultivated studded with graceful images. The whole being finely drawn and painted being done by the United Judgment of Laguerre and GK. The poetic description is fine with several allusions to painting.
> Duchess of Marlborough at l, Duchess of Ormonde, Queen Anne $\frac{1}{2}$ l
> St. Catherine—and several others of Sir Godfrey's own pictures at length and his lady sitting—fine noble picture.'

Thus Godfrey Kneller lived with works of his own masters—Rubens, Rembrandt and Van Dyck—besides his family, for the *St. Catherine* was, like his picture of *St. Agnes*, modelled on his daughter. The *Roman Amphitheatre* is the picture which has given rise to the belief that the brothers visited Rome again in 1677, but this we have already explained.

Godfrey Kneller soon took a lively interest in parish affairs, and despite his irreligious outlook on life he signed the Parish Register on 20th November 1712. On 6th April next year he was appointed Parish Church Warden, but three days later the church at Twickenham fell down and the new Warden immediately took steps to rebuild it. With John James the Architect, Godfrey was largely responsible for the bright chancel which is to be seen to-day attached to the old tower, all that remains of the original church.

The following year he was appointed Vicar's Warden, an appointment he seems to have held until 1st July 1716 when he last signed the vestry minutes— during this period his signature appears some twenty times. His religious ardour —or his desire to be the 'squire,' which I suspect was his real motive—may have waned a little as he grew old.

During this period, in 1714, the year before Mar's Rebellion, he painted both Lord Mar, known as Bobbing John (83), and his wife (2); these very fine pictures are still at Alloa. Queen Anne died in 1714. In May of the following year Godfrey was created a Baronet by George I, but doubtless this elevation had been approved by Anne before her death. Godfrey was the first painter to receive this honour— the highest yet accorded to a painter except in the case of Leighton, the P.R.A. of the last century, who was created a Baron. The degree of Baronet had been created over one hundred years before, in 1611, and Godfrey was the first artist

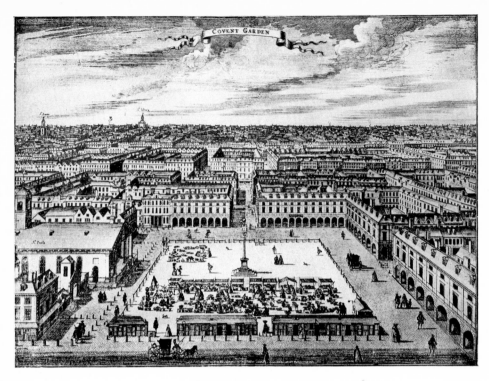

81. COVENT GARDEN

Kneller lived in a house on the right-hand side, at the top

From a print by Sutton Nicholls (1720)

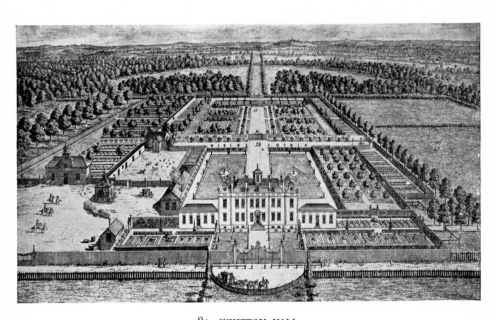

82. WHITTON HALL

Built by Kneller, who lived there from 1711 until his death in 1723

From an engraving by J. Kip in The Borough Library, Twickenham

83. JOHN, 6TH EARL OF MAR, AND HIS SON (1715)

The Earl of Mar and Kellie, K.T., Alloa

so honoured, though many before had been made knights. He painted the coronation picture of George I (69), also the Prince of Wales, later to be king (68).

While at Twickenham, besides being appointed a Deputy Lieutenant for
Middlesex, Godfrey was created a Justice of the Peace. It was in this capacity
that we know of his humanity by the treatment of the master and servant case
and the paupers. On another occasion he found the local constable bringing
before him some people who had had a row. Instead of adjudicating, he told them
all to adjourn to the local ale-house and discuss it over a drink, with the result
that the row was soon settled.

William III had given Godfrey a grant of some £200 a year, but it appears
that he never claimed this. George I, with whom Godfrey remained in favour,
retaining the post of Gentleman of the Privy Chamber, an honour at first given
him by William, resettled the amount on him.

1715 had seen the end of another Stuart claim to the throne. The defeat of
Mar at Sheriffmuir, the failure of the Old Pretender's landing and the death of
Louis XIV that year had made the Stuart restoration impossible; there was a
feeling of security and confidence in the country. As far back as 1711 a Company
had been formed to secure trade in the South Seas, and in 1711 the Company
offered to take over the National Debt which had been created in the reign of
William III to finance his French and Irish wars. The Company proposed to
pay seven millions to buy out the Debt, the Government accepted, and the
Directors thought that the close connection which would result between the
Company and the Government—its sole creditor—would be a great asset. So it
was: everyone bought shares. Small capitalists and corporate bodies such as the
Canton of Berne all subscribed. Shares went up 100 per cent. A tremendous
amount of speculation followed and then came reaction. The South Sea Bubble
burst and the investors lost fortunes. Kneller could afford to lose some £20,000 in
the South Sea Bubble, but when he died some four years later his will left capital
to realise an income of some £2000 per annum. The South Sea Bubble led to the
fall of the Ministry and the rise of Sir Robert Walpole. Leading members of the
Kit Kat, such as Stanhope, were deeply involved. It is of interest to us to know
that the painter could afford to lose so much, and apparently without it making
much difference to his purse.

During this time Godfrey, who would drive about in a coach-and-six, would
often be seen travelling across Hounslow Heath. On one of these journeys in
October 1718 he was attacked by highwaymen and robbed of some £20 and a
gold watch—luckily that was all he had about him at the time.

When he was seventy-three it appears that he was taken ill, and this may
have been the beginning of the decline.

James Craggs wrote to Pope from the Cockpit on 1st October 1719:

'I was yesterday morning out of town, and came directly here this morning where I
received your letter enclosed in a very fine one from Sir Godfrey Kneller. You will easily
imagine how much I am concerned at the accident which had befallen him, but I comfort

myself since his hand and his head which I could least have spared, remain in their former vigour and condition. I do not see why this misfortune is to be completed by the loss of Dr. Arbuthnot and your good company which you will give me leave to expect to-morrow at Battersea, when we will drink Sir Godfrey's health, and make a new appointment against his recovery.—I am, dear Sir . . .'

One of the last fine portraits painted by Kneller was probably his *Countess of Mar* (1715), the residue of the Kit Kat series completed by 1717. From then onwards his painting declined in force. In his last pictures, such as his *William, Earl Cowper*, which, though later inscribed as of 1717, was in fact painted in 1722, in the National Portrait Gallery (86), the firm line and colour have gone; all that is left is the rather pathetic tremble and wash of an old man.

Kneller was taken ill with a fever at the end of 1722. On 27th April of the following year he remade his will and died on 7th November following at his house at Great Queen Street. Pope visited him two days before his death and wrote:

'I paid Sir Godfrey Kneller a visit but two days before he died; I think I never saw a scene of so much vanity in my life. He was lying in bed and contemplating the plan he had made for his own monument. He said many gross things in relation to himself and the memory he would leave behind him. He said he would not like to be among the rascals at Westminster. A memorial there would be sufficient and desired me to write an epitaph for it. I did so afterwards and I think it is the worst thing I ever wrote in my life.'

It was upon this occasion that the following conversation is said to have occurred.

Pope remarked: 'I believe, Sir Godfrey, if Almighty God had had your assistance, the world would have been formed more perfect.'

To which Sir Godfrey replied: 'For God, sire, I believe so too.'

Also at the same time when Pope was sitting beside Sir Godfrey in his sick-bed he told him that he had been a very good man and would therefore be certain to go to a better place. 'I wish God would let me stay at Whitton,' replied Kneller. Godfrey died at Great Queen Street on 7th November 1723. Some two years later, on 6th July 1725, Pope wrote to Lord Stafford describing his last visit thus:

'*July* 1725,

Sir Godfrey sent for me just before he dy'd. He began by telling me he was now convinc'd he could not live; and fell into a passion of tears. I said I hoped he might, but yet if not, he knew it was ye will of God, and would therefore do his best to resign himself to it. He answered with great emotion "No, no, no, it is the evil spirit." The next word he said was this "By God, I will not be buried in Westminster." I asked him why not? He answered "they do bury fools there." Then he said to me "My good friend where will you be buried?" I said "wherever I drop; very likely in Twitnam." He replied "so will I" then proceeded to desire I would write his epitaph which I promised him. It would be endless to tell your Lordship the strange things he suggested on that head; it must be in Latin that all foreigners may read it; it must be in English too etc., I desired him to be easy in all that matter, I w'd certainly do the best that I c'd. Then he desired me that I would take down my father's monument. For it was the best place in ye church to be seen at a distance. This (as y'r

L'dship may well imagine) surprised me quite. I hesitated and said I fear'd it w'd be indecent and y't my mother must be asked as well as I. He fell crying again, and seem'd so violently moved, that in pure humanity to a dying man (as well as to one I thought noncompos) I w'd not directly persist in denying it strongly, but begg'd him to be easy upon ye whole and said I would do all for him that I could with decency. These words and the reserve I can swear to, but y'r Lordship may see ye whole fact (represented upon my word with ye strictest truth) upon which this idle woman (Lady K.) w'd ground her answer of which I was accidently informed by Mr. Pigot.'

I quote from this letter now, for not only does it elaborate on the death-bed scene but it is a clue to what became known to Pope's biographers as 'The Great Tomb Trouble.'

Godfrey was reputed to have been buried at Twickenham on 7th November. His body was certainly taken down there on that day, but where he was actually buried is not known. Mist's *Journal*, as quoted by Vertue, says he was to be buried in Twickenham and describes the funeral procession 'out of town.'

The Twickenham Parish Register has an entry under November 1723:

'I Sir Godfrey Kneller, Baronet, Pay'd the Penalty of the Act.'

What 'paying the penalty' meant is not certain, but it may well hold the clue to the actual place of burial. One school of thought believes that this payment refers to the fine of £5 imposed by the 'Act 30 Charles II' for the use of any material other than sheep's wool in the shroud or lining of the coffin, while the refusal to use a woollen shroud carried the further penalty of burial in unconsecrated ground; of this Pope wrote:

'Odious, in woolen, twould a saint provoke
Were the last words poor Narcissa spoke.'

Cockayne's *Complete Baronetage* says that Kneller was buried in his garden at Whitton. As there is no trace in the graveyard of his being buried there, I feel that it may well have been that he was not buried in a woollen shroud and therefore buried outside the churchyard in the Whitton garden. If this was the case it may have been Lady Kneller's choice, for though a parson's daughter we have no reason to believe that she was any more religious than her husband.

Another view is that the 'penalty' was the levy of Burial Tax, but this was in no way a penalty. I think one day his grave will be found in the garden at Whitton.

Lady Kneller after her husband's death started the trouble with Pope. The latter's father had died in 1717 and Pope had erected a monument to him in Twickenham Church. Lady Kneller asserted that on his death-bed Sir Godfrey had approached Pope and arranged with him that this should be taken down to make way for one eight feet wide to commemorate her husband, as then it was the best place in the church for a monument to be seen at a distance.

We have seen the account of the interview: now we find Pope writing:

'This surprised me quite. I hesitated and said I feared it would be indecent and that my mother must be asked as well as I.'

It appears that Lady Kneller burst into tears and Pope agreed to do what he could with decency. After talking to his mother and considering the matter Pope very naturally refused, as we see in the letter to Stafford. Lady Kneller tried to induce the Church Authorities to interfere, but they also refused and she went to law. Needless to say, she lost. Pope's reason for writing to Stafford was that the monument to Pope's father was over the Stafford pew.

There is no monument to Kneller in Twickenham Church, and some authorities, such as Thorne in his *London*, say that the Pope-Kneller row was the cause of this. There were certainly other sites in the church, as can be seen to-day, and, had Lady Kneller so wished, a monument could have been erected in another place; the absence seems to bear out further the view that Kneller was not buried there.

In his will Kneller left £300 for his own memorial, and though he was not to be buried in Westminster Abbey, with 'the fools,' a monument by Rysbrack was erected to him there. It shows both his own bust and the profile of Lady Kneller on a medallion and is placed very high on the north wall of the choir behind the stalls; visitors can easily miss it unless they ask. He is the only painter who is commemorated in the Abbey (84).

The inscription reads:

'Godefredi Kneller Equitis Rom. Imp. et Angliæ
Baronetti Pictoris Regibus Carolo II, Jacobi II,
Gulielmo III, Annæ Reginæ, Georgio I, qui obit.'

The epitaph by Pope follows:

'Kneller, by Heaven and not a master taught,
Whose art was nature and whose pictures thought;
Now for two ages having snatched from fate
Whate'er was beauteous, or whate'er was great,
Rests crown'd with Princes' Honours, Poets' Lays,
Due to his merit and brave Thirst of Praise;
Living, great Nature fear'd he might outvie
Her works; and, dying, fears herself may die.'

No wonder after Lady Kneller had tried to oust his father's monument that Pope regretted this epitaph, which was certainly very fulsome. The last couplet was taken from Raphael's, which runs

'Raphael, timuit, quo sospite, vinci,
Rerum magna parens et moriente, mori.'

At least Godfrey Kneller would have liked this praise, but Johnson in his Life of Pope in his *Poets* was not quite so fulsome about the lines. His comment runs:

'Of this epitaph the first couplet is good, the second not so bad, and the third is deformed with a broken metaphor, the word crowned not being applicable to honours or lays, and the fourth is not only borrowed from the epitaph on Raphael, but of very harsh construction.'

84. KNELLER MONUMENT IN WESTMINSTER ABBEY
    BY RYSBRACK

85. KNELLER—IVORY MEDALLION (attributed to
    Jean Cavalier)

National Portrait Gallery

86. LORD CHANCELLOR COWPER (1722)

National Portrait Gallery

The only account of Kneller's funeral procession is in Vertue and we have no record of the expense; but his loss was felt in the world of art and society.

To give some idea of his popularity and position there appeared from the house of the printer J. Roberts in 1725 a poem entitled *A Session of Painters Occasioned by the Death of the Late Sir Godfrey Kneller*, and inscribed to his widow, of which I will quote the introduction and its twenty verses, for it shows the esteem in which he was held, as well as being a rhymed obituary and review of contemporary painting.

'Each heavenly piece unwearied we compare
Match Raphael's grace with thy lov'd Guido's air
Caracci's strength, Correggio's softer line
Paulo's free stroke, and Titian's warmth divine
Yet still how faint, by Precept is expressed
The living image in the painter's breast?
Thence endless stream of fair ideas flow
Strike in the sketch and in the picture glow.

Mourn, England, mourn, since Kneller is no more,
    Who shall his place supply?
What genius can the mighty art restore,
    Or must it vacant lie?
Alas already is the laurel given
Before Apelles can descend from heaven.

But soon the God with all his train came down
    And thus his will proclaimed:
I come (said he) to give the vacant crown;
    He must by me be named.
He that usurps it ne'er was known to me,
Merit shall wear the wreath by my decree.

No sooner had the God these words declared
    But straight whole troops came in,
Some wondrous fine, and some distressed appeared,
    Yet vainly great within;
These noisy sons of fame a war declare,
Pallates and pencils brandish in the air.

Apelles starting at this numerous sight
    With angry voice thus said:
To flourish signs, and sign posts is your right,
    Be gone and mind your trade.
Let candidates of worth have room to please
None but of worth shall the deceas'd succeed.

A sly short cringing creature first appeared
    And cried with abject mein:
Great Kneller was my tutor, most revered
    I wiped his pencils clean.

Apelles gravely eyed th' industrious thing,
Though you can't paint, I hear that you can sing.

This said, grave Ph— bowed with courtly air
    And vainly thus laid claim;
A genius only shou'd this laurel wear
    Some chosen son of fame.
Apelles stopp'd him short and frowning said
Presumptuous man, be satisfied with bread.

H—r, a famous city candidate
    Came puffing out his breath.
Wish not (Apelles cried) a better fate
    Than daubing tasteless wretch;
Content thyself to please ill judging sinners,
To get their money and devour their dinners.

Stiff as his works elaborate G— came,
    And thus began to sue;
The greatest nobles long have known my fame,
    Nor is strange to you.
The God replied, thy hand preferred should be
Had it more praise from others, less from thee.

A rich old sage to prove his boasted skill
    To draw a portrait tried,
When! strange! his pencil changed into a quill.
    Apelles smiling cried:
You paint almost as ill as you indite
And yet you draw much worse than you can write.

Apelles smiled to see his favourite son,
    Come pressing through the throng.
Proceed (cried out the God) as you've begun
    Forget the dance and song;
With haste thy rough unpolished ways refine
And grow the ladies' darling, as thou'rt mine.

The God's piercing eye soon Smy—t saw
    With Dy—r by his side.
Thy merit Smy—t hust applause will draw,
    Apelles smiling cried
In Dy—r both the sister arts agree
To please in painting, and in poetry.

Apelles wav'd his hand with graceful air
    To an old modest sage.
'Tis just (he cry'd) that I this truth declare
    To his ill judging age;
Thy judgment I approve, go on, be great!
'Tis sure some merit well to imitate.

Here paused the God—and viewing well each rank
 Thus spake with eager voice:
Why do I miss my favourite Van . . . k?
 He long has been my choice,
Oft have I said if he with Kneller's care
Would progress make, he might his loss repair.

But soon quick envy reached Apelles' ears
 And babbling joyful told,
Want, is the reason why he not appears,
 Not vanity but gold.
'Tis wealth alone that builds the surest name
He feeds on airy food, that lives on fame.

Upon Apelles' brow there sat a cloud
 Which his displeasure spoke;
Slowly he rose, and to the gaping crowd
 He thus his silence broke:
Ye candidates for fame, attention give,
From my impartial hand your fates receive.

Some few I know who are not in this throng
 Whose merits I approve,
Nor would I do their modest prudence wrong,
 Because they have not strove,
With vain impertinent attempts, to share
A wreath, they know they are not fit to wear.

Observe my Kneller, mark his virtues well
 How just a draught he drew.
He strove Van Dyck and Lilly to excel,
 His comprehensive view
Held all the noble theory complete
Wise yet not vain, exalted yet discreet.

His matchless Art by nature's force display'd
 Are in those portraits shown;
Observe that fine expression, light and shade
 The features well are known
His men with awful grace the eye control
His women touch the heart and charm the soul.

Now where's that vain ambitious man, that will
 With mighty Kneller vie
And not confess his much superior skill,
 Whose works will never die?
But oh! no merit, wealth, nor power can save
The greatest mortal from the certain grave.

My fav'rite son pursue his tracts with care
    And thus true nature know,
You must his taste enjoy, his judgment share
    And with his spirit glow,
Till one thus shines to match the mighty dead
The wreath shall stay on the Deo Facto's head.
This said he upwards took his flight,
Streaking the cloudy paths with beam of light.'

Kneller's will is dated 27th April 1723, with a codicil of 24th October—about the day Pope visited him. He left a fortune of about £2000 per annum which included, besides the Great Queen Street homes and Whitton, property at Reigate in Surrey and in Wild Street, London. The chief beneficiaries were his widow and his daughter Agnes, but he also left legacies to the daughters of his brother Andrew at Hamburg. His daughter's son, Godfrey Huckle, was made a legatee provided he took the name Kneller, which he did by Act of Parliament in 1731.

Edward Byng was another beneficiary, and he was ordered to finish or perfect any pictures in agreement with Lady Kneller, to whom all portraits, finished and unfinished, were left. There were about 800 of these, and Byng had to be subservient to the widow; no portraits were to be sold for less than the regular price; they were nearly all put on the market, which accounts for many bad attributions of contemporary pictures. Byng was to get half the price of the pictures he finished.

Lady Kneller died at Twickenham on 11th December 1729. After her death the house at Whitton became the residence of Sir Samuel Prine. He sold it to a Mr. Calvert, who had the house enlarged and remodelled under Philip Hardwick. It was then that the last trace of Kneller, including the staircase, probably disappeared and the outside was refaced as it is to-day. In 1847 it was purchased by the Council of Education as a Training College for Workhouse Schoolmasters—the first master being Dr. Temple, subsequently Head Master of Rugby, Bishop of London and Archbishop of Canterbury. Eleven years later it was taken over by the War Office as a Training School for army bandsmen, and was used during the 1939-45 war as G.H.Q. for Home forces, and from it the Battle of Britain was fought.

Godfrey Huckle was a lucky man, for not only did he become his godfather Godfrey's heir but he married a Mary Weekes, the daughter of Luke Weekes of Donhead Hall, Wiltshire, and here the descendants of the Kneller family lived until the beginning of the last century, as is shown by the family tree in Appendix A.

In 1825 Godfrey John Kneller sold the Donhead property to a Charles Wyndham. Godfrey John Kneller had a son Godfrey Hasting Graeme Kneller, born in 1815, who had no family. Godfrey John's brother, John Fullager Kneller, had descendants, and the head of the family to-day is Oliver Godfrey

Kneller, who married his first cousin, Vera St. John Kneller, whose grandmother was a daughter of a Lord Bolingbroke, a descendant of the great St. John, Kneller's friend, whom he painted.

Godfrey Kneller's brother's family flourished in Hamburg, but the war has prevented my researches in tracing them. They would, however, be of little interest to our quest, for of his early life we know what we require and it was in England that Godfrey made his name.

APPENDIX A

KNELLER FAMILY TREE

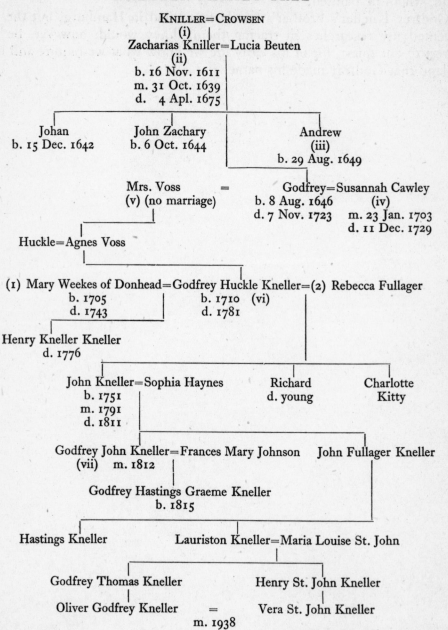

KNILLER=CROWSEN
(i)

Zacharias Kniller=Lucia Beuten
(ii)
b. 16 Nov. 1611
m. 31 Oct. 1639
d. 4 Apl. 1675

Johan
b. 15 Dec. 1642

John Zachary
b. 6 Oct. 1644

Andrew
(iii)
b. 29 Aug. 1649

Mrs. Voss   =   Godfrey=Susannah Cawley
(v) (no marriage)   b. 8 Aug. 1646   (iv)
d. 7 Nov. 1723   m. 23 Jan. 1703
d. 11 Dec. 1729

Huckle=Agnes Voss

(1) Mary Weekes of Donhead=Godfrey Huckle Kneller=(2) Rebecca Fullager
b. 1705   b. 1710 (vi)
d. 1743   d. 1781

Henry Kneller Kneller
d. 1776

John Kneller=Sophia Haynes
b. 1751
m. 1791
d. 1811

Richard
d. young

Charlotte
Kitty

Godfrey John Kneller=Frances Mary Johnson
(vii)   m. 1812

John Fullager Kneller

Godfrey Hastings Graeme Kneller
b. 1815

Hastings Kneller

Lauriston Kneller=Maria Louise St. John

Godfrey Thomas Kneller

Henry St. John Kneller

Oliver Godfrey Kneller   =   Vera St. John Kneller
m. 1938

(i) Owned Estate near Halle, Saxony. Surveyor of Mines to Count Mansfeldt.
(ii) Employed by Queen Eleanor in Sweden. Settled and married at Lübeck.
(iii) Afterwards Organist at St. Catherine's, Lübeck, and St. Peter's, Hamburg.
(iv) Daughter of Rector of Henley-on-Thames.
(v) Hanoverian wife of a Quaker whom Kneller bought. Not married.
(vi) Assumed name Kneller by Act of Parliament, 1731.
(vii) Sold Donhead Hall in 1825 to Charles Wyndham.

APPENDIX B

CHRONOLOGICAL CATALOGUE OF SOME OF GODFREY KNELLER'S PRINCIPAL WORKS WHICH CAN BE ATTRIBUTED AND DATED

1668	Aged Student (Copernicus) Cornelius Bruyn	Lübeck Town Library Rijks Museum, Amsterdam
1672/73	Cardinal Bassadona Self-Portrait	Rome Victoria and Albert Museum

1673	Mayor Heinrich
	Senator Frederick B. Rodder
	Senator Th. Fredenhagen
	Frau Fredenhagen
		St. Catherine's, Lübeck
		      ,, ,,
		Private Collection
		    ,, ,,

1675	Zacharias Kneller	Maria Church, Lübeck
1676/77	James Vernon (9)	National Portrait Gallery
1679/80	Duke of Monmouth Mary Smith	Boughton (Duke of Buccleuch) Engraving (British Museum)
1682	William, 5th Earl of Bedford Sir John Micklethwaite Michael Dahl	Woburn (Duke of Bedford) Royal College of Physicians Engraving
1683	Sir Charles Cotterell	Rousham
1684	Sir Thomas Allen Duke of Monmouth Charles II Samuel Pepys (10)	Greenwich (Maritime Museum) Alloa (Earl of Mar and Kellie) Alloa 1. Royal Society 2. Magdalene, Cambridge
1685	Godfrey Kneller (30) John Evelyn Anne, Duchess of Leeds Charles, Earl Halifax Louis XIV	Knowsley (Earl of Derby) Hitchin (R. Delme Radcliffe) Holkham (Earl of Leicester) National Portrait Gallery Drayton (Col. K. Stopford Sackville)
1686	Queen Mary of Modena Rachel and Catherine Russell Wriothesley, 2nd Duke of Bedford (45) Crucifixion (43)	Hampton Court Woburn ,, Anglesey (Lord Fairhaven)
1687	Thomas Lamplough Louise, Duchess of Portsmouth Ferdinando d'Adda William, Earl of Bedford Rev. Mr. Child	Queen's College, Oxford Sherborne (Col. F. Wingfield Digby) Petworth (Earl of Leconfield) Woburn Osterley (Earl of Jersey)

P*

1687	Henrietta and Anne Churchill	Althorp (Earl Spencer)
	Sir Christopher Wren (57)	Royal Society
	Mrs. Voss and Child (28)	Engraving
	The Chinese Convert (1)	Kensington Palace
1688	Duchess of Portsmouth	Holkham
1689	Henry Aldrich	Christ Church, Oxford
	John Evelyn (11)	Royal Society
	James II (12)	St. James's Palace
	Anthony Leigh (24)	Garrick Club and National Portrait Gallery
	Samuel Pepys	Greenwich
	Isaac Newton (22)	Kensington Palace
1690	Sir George Mackenzie	Bodleian
	William III (66) and Mary II (67)	St. James's Palace
1691	Archbishop Tillotson	Lambeth Palace
1691/92	Hampton Court Beauties (14-21)	Hampton Court
1692	Charles, Earl of Euston	Euston (Duke of Grafton)
1693	Dr. Thomas Burnett	Charterhouse
1694	Mrs. Wrey	Hatfield (Marquess of Salisbury)
	Ralph Bathurst	Trinity College, Oxford
	Charles, 6th Earl of Dorset	Knole (Lord Sackville)
	Elizabeth, Lady Latimer	Hatfield (Marquess of Salisbury)
1695	Lord Tavistock	Woburn
	Anne Howland	"
	John Dryden	National Portrait Gallery
	Godert, Earl of Athlone (23)	National Gallery, Dublin
1696	Sir Thomas Southwell (53)	Royal Society
	Italian Greyhound (50)	St. James's Palace (Sir Godfrey Thomas)
1697	Peter the Great (75)	Kensington Palace
	William of Orange (25)	Hampton Court, Leningrad, National Gallery, Dublin, etc.
	Countess of Salisbury	Hatfield
	James, 2nd Duke of Queensberry	Alloa
	Elector of Bavaria	Buckingham Palace
	William, 1st Earl of Portland	Welbeck (Duke of Portland)
1698	Joost Van Keppel, 1st Earl of Albemarle (54)	National Portrait Gallery
	Nathaniel, Lord Carew	Bodleian and Lincoln College, Oxford
1699	Earl of Salisbury	Hatfield
1700	Henry Sydney, Earl of Romney	National Portrait Gallery
	Lady M. and Viscount Villiers	Middleton (Earl of Jersey)
1701	Vice-Admiral John Benbow	Greenwich
	John Wallis	Bodleian

1702	Isaac Newton	National Portrait Gallery
	Anne Oldfield (55)	Garrick Club
1703	Charles, Archduke of Austria	Kensington Palace
	Queen Anne (26)	St. James's Palace
	Thomas Betterton (62)	Garrick Club and Knole
1704	John Locke (70)	Christ Church and Royal Society
	Admiral George Churchill	Greenwich
1705	Prince George of Denmark and George Clarke	All Souls, Oxford
	Sir John Jennings	Greenwich
1705	Sarah, Duchess of Marlborough	Petworth
1706/7	Admiral Series	Greenwich
1708	Rachel, Duchess of Beaufort	Euston
	Henry, Marquess of Worcester	,,
	Sir Jonathan Trelawney	Christ Church
	George Byng, Viscount Torrington	Greenwich
1709	William Congreve (73)	National Portrait Gallery (Kit Kat)
	John, Duke of Montagu	,, ,, ,, ,,
	Evelyn, Duke of Kingston	,, ,, ,, ,,
1710	Charles, Earl of Halifax	Kit Kat
	Duke of Marlborough	Blenheim (Duke of Marlborough)
1711	Sir Christopher Wren	National Portrait Gallery
1712	Dr. John Radcliffe	Radcliffe Library, Oxford
1713	James, 2nd Duke of Ormonde	National Gallery, Dublin
	Lady Jane Smyth (56)	Nottingham Art Gallery
	Charles, 6th Duke of Somerset	Petworth
1714	Henrietta Cavendish Holles, Countess of Oxford	Welbeck and Christ Church
	Thomas, Earl of Macclesfield	National Portrait Gallery
	Lord Percy Seymour	Petworth
1714/15	Frances, Countess of Mar (2)	Alloa
	Earl of Mar and son (83)	,,
1715	William, Lord Digby	Magdalen College, Oxford
	George I (69)	St. James's Palace
	William Wycherley (5)	Knole
	Henry, Viscount Bolingbroke	Petworth
	Thomas Hopkins	National Portrait Gallery (Kit Kat)
	Joseph Addison	Engraving
1716	Classical Painting (44)	Cirencester (Earl Bathurst)
	Frances Thynne, Duchess of Somerset	Petworth
	George II as Prince of Wales (68)	Trinity College, Dublin
1717	William Pulteney, Earl of Bath	National Portrait Gallery (Kit Kat)
	Richard Lumley, Earl of Scarborough	,, ,, ,, ,,
	Robert Boyle, Viscount Shannon (78)	,, ,, ,, ,,
	Jacob Tonson (77)	,, ,, ,, ,,
	Queen Caroline, with son Cumberland	Kensington Palace
	George, Lord Willoughby de Broke	,, ,,

1718	Bishop Atterbury	Christ Church, Oxford
1719	Edward Harley, Earl of Oxford	
1720	Self-Portrait (33)	Bodleian
1722	William, Earl Cowper (86)	National Portrait Gallery
1723	Alexander Pope (72)	Engraving

APPENDIX D 1

CATALOGUE OF MEZZOTINTS AFTER KNELLER

1. Thomas Beard
    i Jane, Countess of Clarendon

2. Isaac Beckett (1653-1715)
   Worked 1681-88
    i Madam Baker
    ii Charles II   (a)
    iii   ,,   (b)
    iv Barbara, Duchess of Cleveland
    v Elizabeth, Lady Croyton
    vi William, Earl of Devonshire
    vii Catherine, Countess of Dorchester
    viii Robert Fielding
    ix Henry, Duke of Grafton
    x Isabella, Duchess of Grafton
    xi James, Duke of York
    xii James II
    xiii Godfrey Kneller
    xiv Madam Lawson
    xv Charlotte, Countess of Lichfield   (a)
    xvi   ,,   ,,   ,,   (b)
    xvii Mary of Modena
    xviii John, Earl of Melfort
    xix John, Earl of Mulgrave
    xx Louise, Duchess of Portsmouth
    xxi Lawrence, Earl of Rochester
    xxii Wriothesley, Lord Russell (45)
    xxiii Mme. Soames
    xxiv Sir James Tillie
    xxv Mme. Turner
    xxvi Thomas Worsley
    xxvii Mrs. Henrietta Maria Yarborough
    xxviii Lady unknown
    xxix Peter John Potemkin (63)

3. Abraham Blooteling (1634-1695)
   Worked 1673-76
    Peter John Potemkin

4. G. Bockman
    Charles, Earl of Peterborough

5. John Brooks
    William III

6. J. Cooper
    James II

7. R. Cooper (d. 1764)
    John, Earl of Stair

8. W. Dickinson (1723-1746)
    Master Montagu

9. John Dixon (1740-1780)
    Lady Jane Clifford

10. William Emmet
    i Queen Anne
    ii Prince George of Denmark

11. John Esplens (d. 1743)
    Sir Isaac Newton

12. John Faber (Senior) (d. 1721)

    i Admiral George Byng
   ii John Dryden (4)
  iii William Talbot *(a)*
   iv   ,,   ,,   *(b)*
    v John Wallis

13. John Faber (Junior)
    Worked 1712-1756

    i Sir John Fortescue Aland
   ii Princess Anne
  iii Hampton Court Beauties
      a Godfrey Kneller (13)
      b Mary II
      c Isabella, Duchess of Grafton
      d Dodington, Duchess of Manchester
      e Sarah, Duchess of Marlborough
      f Diana, Duchess of St. Albans
      g Jane, Countess of Clarendon
      h Mary, Countess of Dorset
      i Mary, Countess of Essex
      j Carey, Countess of Peterborough
      k Margaret, Countess of Ranelagh
      l Anne, Lady Middleton
      m Mrs. Scroop
   iv Louisa, Countess of Berkeley
    v Rachel, Lady Bradshaigh
   vi Rev. Thomas Burnett
  vii Admiral George Byng
 viii Queen Caroline
   ix   ,,   ,,
    x Joseph Carreras
   xi Francis Couplet
  xii Nathaniel, Lord Crew
 xiii George Arutin
  xiv George I
  xv Prince of Wales *(a)*
  xvi   ,,   ,,   *(b)*
 xvii Margaret, Lady Hardwicke
xviii James II—half-length
  xix Anne, Countess of Jersey
  xx Kit Kat Club
        Godfrey Kneller
        Charles, Duke of Somerset
        Charles, Duke of Richmond
        Charles, Duke of Grafton (34)
        William, Duke of Devonshire
        John, Duke of Marlborough
        John, Duke of Montagu
        Evelyn, Duke of Kingston
        Thomas, Duke of Newcastle
        Henry, Earl of Lincoln
        Charles, Duke of Manchester
        Lionel, Duke of Dorset
        Thomas, Marquess of Wharton
        Theophilus, Earl of Huntingdon
        Charles, Earl of Dorset
        Algernon, Earl of Essex
        Charles, Earl of Carlisle

13. John Faber (Junior)—*contd.*

xx Kit Kat Club—*contd.*

Richard, Earl of Burlington
James, Earl of Berkeley
Richard, Earl of Scarborough
Francis, Earl of Godolphin
Charles, Earl of Halifax
James, Earl Stanhope
Spencer, Earl of Wilmington
Richard, Viscount Cobham
Charles, Lord Mohun (80)
Charles, Lord Cornwallis
John, Earl of Carbery
John, Lord Somers
Richard, Viscount Shannon
Sir Robert Walpole (Earl of Orford)
Sir John Vanbrugh (64)
Sir Samuel Garth
Sir Richard Steele
John Tidcombe
William Pulteney (Earl of Bath)
Joseph Addison
George Stepney
Abraham Stanyan
John Dormer
Edmund Dunch
William Walsh
William Congreve
Charles Dartiquenave (79)
Thomas Hopkins
Edward Hopkins
Arthur Maynwaring
Jacob Tonson

xxi Mrs. Knight
xxii Sir John Leake
xxiii Mary, Countess of Macclesfield
xxiv John, Duke of Marlborough
xxv Mary, Duchess of Montagu
xxvi Sir James Montagu
xxvii Thomas, Duke of Newcastle
xxviii Thomas, Lord Parker
xxix Alexander Pope (72)
xxx Matthew Prior
xxxi Michael Richards
xxxii John Sabine
xxxiii Sir Hans Sloane
xxxiv Sir John Tillotson
xxxv John Wyck
xxxvi Lady in Meditation

14. William Faithorne

i Mary II
ii John Moore
iii James, Duke of Ormonde
iv William III   (*a*) (66)
v   „   (*b*)
vi   „   (*c*)

15. Michael Forde

i William III
ii William III and Schomberg

16. Edward Fisher (1730-1785)   J. Baptiste Monnoyer

17. Gerard   John, Duke of Marlborough

18. John Gisbourne   Sir Henry Hatsell

19. John Griffier (1645-1718)   James II

20. William Humphrey (1740- c. 1795)   Richard King

21. Thomas Johnson (1708-1767)   Thomas, Marquess of Wharton

22. Francis Kyte
    i Henrietta, Countess of Godolphin
    ii Harriett, Duchess of Newcastle
    iii Sir Thomas Parker (a)
    iv   „   „   (b)

23. Bernard Lens (1659-1725)   Isabella, Duchess of Grafton

24. E. Luttrell (1650-1710)   William, Lord Russell

25. James McCardell (1729-1765)   Lionel, Duke of Dorset

26. A. Miller
    i Lübeck
    ii John, Duke of Marlborough
    iii Sir Isaac Newton
    iv Frederick, Duke of Schomberg
    v John Tillotson
    vi William III (a)
    vii   „   „   (b)

27. John Oliver (1616-1701)
    i James II
    ii George, Lord Jeffreys

28. Peter Pelham (1680-1751)
    i Princess Anne
    ii John, Lord Carteret
    iii Hon. Spencer Compton
    iv George I
    v James, Duke of Ormonde
    vi Thomas, Duke of Newcastle

29. Richard Purcell
    i William III
    ii William III and Schomberg

30. William Sherwin (1650-1714)   Henry, Duke of Beaufort

31. John Simon (1675-1755)
    i Joseph Addison
    ii Queen Anne (a) (26)
    iii   „   „   (b)
    iv Princess Anne
    v Francis Atterbury
    vi John, Earl of Carbery
    vii Queen Caroline
    viii Thomas, Earl of Coventry
    ix James Craggs (65)
    x John, Lord Cutts
    xi Charles, Earl of Dorset
    xii Thomas Earl
    xiii Prince Eugene
    xiv Sir Samuel Garth
    xv George I (69)
    xvi Prince of Wales (George II)
    xvii Simon, Lord Harcourt
    xviii Arthur Maynwaring
    xix Lord Morley

31. John Simon (1675-1755)—*contd.*

    xx Sir Isaac Newton (like Smith) (*a*)
   xxi   ,,   ,,   (*b*)
  xxii Margaret, Lady North (*a*)
 xxiii   ,,   ,,   ,,   (*b*)
 xxiv Robert, Earl of Oxford
  xxv Sir Thomas Parker
 xxvi Charles, Earl of Peterborough
 xxvii William Pulteney
xxviii John, Lord Somers
 xxix Charles, Duke of Somerset
  xxx James, Earl Stanhope
 xxxi Sir Richard Steele
 xxxii Charles, Earl of Sunderland
xxxiii Count Tarouca
xxxiv Sir Richard Temple
 xxxv John Tillotson
xxxvi Charles, Viscount Townsend
xxxvii Sir John Vanbrugh
xxxviii Sir Robert Walpole
xxxix Thomas, Marquess of Wharton
   xl William III

32. John Smith (1654-1720)

     i Arnold Van Keppel, Earl of Albemarle
    ii Henry Aldrich
   iii Anne (as Princess)
   iv Anne (as Queen)—half-length   (*a*)
    v   ,,   ,,   Reverse to 4   (*b*)
   vi   ,,   ,,   half-length oval   (*c*)
  vii   ,,   ,,   Reverse to 6   (*d*)
 viii   ,,   ,,   as 6, but older   (*e*)
   ix Princess Anne—three-quarter-length (*f*)
    x   ,,   ,,   half-length   (*g*)
   xi William Johnson, Marquess of Annandale
  xii Godert de Ginkel, Earl of Athlone
 xiii John, Marquess of Blandford
 xiv Henrietta Crofts, Duchess of Bolton
  xv John, Earl of Bridgwater
 xvi Lionel, Lord Buckhurst, and Lady Mary Sackville
 xvii William, Lord Bury
xviii Mrs. Carter
 xix Hon. Robt. Cecil
  xx Charles II (27)
 xxi Sarah Chicheley
 xxii Henrietta and Anne Churchill
xxiii Richard, Lord Clifford, and Lady Jane Boyle
xxiv William Congreve
 xxv Catherine, Lady Copley
xxvi Mrs. Eleanor Copley
xxvii Nicola Cosimo
xxviii Thomas Coulson
 xxix William, Lord Cowper
  xxx Lady Elizabeth Cromwell (*a*)
 xxxi   ,,   ,,   ,,   (*b*)
 xxxii Mrs. Cross
xxxiii Elizabeth, Lady Cutts
xxxiv Mme. D'Avenant

32. John Smith (1654-1720)—*contd.*

xxxv	Henry, Count D'Auvernquenik	
xxxvi	Henry, Lord Delamere	
xxxvii	William Dolben	
xxxviii	Charles, Earl of Dorset	
xxxix	Mary, Countess of Essex	
xl	Charles, Lord Euston	
xli	John, Earl of Exeter	
xlii	Edward Fowler	
xliii	John, Count Gallas	
xliv	Prince George of Denmark	(a)
xlv	„ „ „	(b)
xlvi	„ „ „	(c)
xlvii	„ „ „	(d)
xlviii	George I (a)	
xlix	„ (b)	
l	Prince of Wales (George II) (a) (68)	
li	„ „ „ (b)	
lii	Grinling Gibbons (71)	
liii	William, Duke of Gloucester	(a)
liv	„ „ „	(b)
lv	„ „ „	(c)
lvi	„ „ „	(d)
lvii	„ „ „	(e)
lviii	Sidney, Earl Godolphin	
lix	Isabella, Duchess of Grafton	
lx	Anthony Henley	
lxi	Edward, Lord Hinchinbroke	
lxii	Sir William Hodges	
lxiii	Mrs. Rachel How	
lxiv	Lady Howard (a)	
lxv	„ „ (b)	
lxvi	Arabella Hunt	
lxvii	James II (a)	
lxviii	„ „ (b)	
lxix	„ „ (c)	
lxx	Sir Godfrey Kneller	
lxxi	Anthony Leigh	
lxxii	Meinhard Schomberg, Duke of Leinster	
lxxiii	John Locke	
lxxiv	Madam Loftus	
lxxv	John Erskine, Earl of Mar	
lxxvi	Griselda, Countess of Marchmont	
lxxvii	Patrick Hume, Earl of Marchmont	
lxxviii	John, Duke of Marlborough	(a)
lxxix	„ „ „	(b)
lxxx	„ „ „	(c)
lxxxi	Sarah, Duchess of Marlborough	(a)
lxxxii	„ „ „	(b)
lxxxiii	Mary of Modena (a)	
lxxxiv	„ „ (b)	
lxxxv	Mary II (a)	
lxxxvi	„ „ (b)	
lxxxvii	Anne, Duchess of Monmouth	
lxxxviii	Essex Mostyn	
lxxxix	Charles Montagu, Earl Halifax	

32. John Smith (1654-1720)—*contd.*

xc John, Earl of Mulgrave (*a*)
xci   ,,   ,,   ,, (*b*)
xcii Sir Isaac Newton
xciii James, Duke of Ormonde (*a*)
xciv   ,,   ,,   ,, (*b*)
xcv   ,,   ,,   ,, (*c*)
xcvi Mary, Duchess of Ormonde
xcvii   ,,   ,,   ,, with her son
xcviii Robert, Earl of Oxford
xcix Sir John Percival
c Alexander Pope
ci Margaret, Countess of Ranelagh
cii William Richards
ciii Peter the First of Russia
civ Catherine, Countess of Rutland
cv Diana, Duchess of St. Albans
cvi Frances, Countess of Salisbury
cvii James, Earl of Salisbury
cviii Mrs. Sally Salisbury (*a*)
cix   ,,   ,,   ,, (*b*)
cx Frederick, Duke of Schomberg
cxi James Ogilvy, Earl of Seafield
cxii Mrs. Sherard
cxiii John Smith (60)
cxiv Edward Southwell
cxv Sir Robert Southwell
cxvi Charles III of Spain (*a*)
cxvii   ,,   ,, smaller (*b*)
cxviii Christopher Walter Stockdale
cxix Prince James Stuart
cxx William Stuckeley
cxxi Thomas Tompion
cxxii Anne, Lady Torrington
cxxiii Thomas Newport, Lord Torrington
cxxiv Charles, Viscount Townshend
cxxv John Hay, Earl of Tweeddale
cxxvi   ,,   ,,   ,, when Marquess
cxxvii William Van der Velde
cxxviii William, Lord Villiers and Lady Mary Villiers
cxxix Mrs. Voss and child (28)
cxxx Miss Voss
cxxxi Miss Voss as St. Agnes (61)
cxxxii Thomas, Marquess of Wharton
cxxxiii Queen Caroline (*a*)
cxxxiv   ,,   ,, (*b*)
cxxxv William III (*a*)
cxxxvi   ,,   ,, (*b*)
cxxxvii   ,,   ,, (*c*)
cxxxviii Dudley Woodbridge: Face and wig
cxxxix Sir Christopher Wren

33. Jonathan Spilsbury   John Locke
34. Samuel Taylor   George II
35. R. Thompson (1693)   George I (as Prince of Hanover)
36. Valentine (1739-1813)   Joseph Carreras

Q

37. John Van der Vaart (1647-1721)   Anne, Duchess of Monmouth
38. Alexander Van Hacken (1701)   George Baillie
    Worked 1735-1740
39. Paul Van Somer (1649-1694)   James II
40. G. White
    i John Dryden
    ii Francis, Earl of Godolphin
    iii Edmund Halley
    iv J. B. Monnoyer (59)
    v Alexander Pope
    vi Mrs. Mary Smith

41. Robert White (1645-1704)
    i Princess Anne
    ii Isabella, Duchess of Grafton
    iii Henry, Duke of Norfolk
    iv James, Duke of Ormonde
    v John, Earl of Radnor
    vi Charles, Duke of Somerset

42. R. Williams (1645-1703)
    i Thomas Betterton (62)
    ii Charles II
    iii Dorothy Cressy
    iv Theophilus, Earl of Huntingdon
    v Lady Harriet Wentworth

43. Engravers not ascertained
    i Lady Bucknell
    ii George, Lord Jeffreys
    iii Madam Knatchbull
    iv Lady Middleton
    v William, Lord Russell
    vi William, Lord Cowper
    vii Mrs. Cross (48)
    viii Prince of Wales (George II)
    ix Alexander Pope
    x Sir Richard Steele